D1711833

Bridging the Communication Gap with the Elderly

Practical Strategies for Caregivers

Barbara J. Cox
Lois Lord Waller

AHA

The views expressed in this publication are strictly those of the authors and do not necessarily represent official positions of the American Hospital Association.

Library of Congress Cataloging-in-Publication Data

Cox, Barbara J.
    Bridging the communication gap with the elderly : practical strategies for caregivers / Barbara J. Cox, Lois Lord Waller.
          p.   cm.
    Includes bibliographical references.
    ISBN 1-55648-080-6
    1. Aged—Care. 2. Communication in medicine. 3. Medical personnel and patient. 4. Geriatrics. I. Waller, Lois. II. Title.
    [DNLM: 1. Communication. 2. Long Term Care—in old age. 3. Long Term Care—methods. 4. Professional-Patient Relations. WT 30 C877b]
RC954.3.C68   1991
362.1'9897—dc20
DNLM/DLC
for Library of Congress   91-31599
                                                   CIP

Catalog no. 130104

© 1991 by Barbara J. Cox and Lois Lord Waller

Printed in the USA

𝔸ℍ𝔸 is a service mark of the American Hospital Association used under license by American Hospital Publishing, Inc., an American Hospital Association company

Text set in Trump Medieval
5M—11/91—0306

Marlene Chamberlain, Project Editor
Nancy Charpentier, Editorial Assistant
Marcia Bottoms, Managing Editor
Peggy DuMais, Production Coordinator
Marcia Kuhr and Luke Smith, Designers
Brian Schenk, Books Division Director

Dedicated to Betty J. Harrington,
a model of care and respect to
people of all ages

Contents

About the Authors

Barbara J. Cox, R.N., received her nursing degree from Seattle University. She is currently the vice-president for mission services of the Dominican Network, a group of hospitals in eastern Washington, where she is responsible for ethics and values education. Her nursing experience includes acute care, long-term care, and hospice home care. A cofounder in 1978 of Hospice of Spokane, Barbara has since become known for her ability to express the need in all of us to make the most of our communication skills with one another. Ms. Cox conducts workshops throughout the West on ethics, grief, and respectful care of older persons.

Lois Lord Waller has a master's degree in communication studies from Colorado State University and has taught English and communications for 20 years in six states and three countries. Mrs. Waller has had extensive editing experience; most recently as senior editor of a West Indian children's magazine. She was executive director of Friend to Friend (a nursing home visitation program) in Spokane, Washington. She was a member of the first United Methodist Pacific Northwest Conference Council on Aging Adults and helped compile and edit its initial survey investigation into the complex nature of the needs of the elderly in churches in the Pacific Northwest. She is currently studying the process of communication with elderly people who cannot respond.

Introduction

In the United States today, according to the U.S. Bureau of the Census, there are 2.9 million people who are 85 years old or older. But the Bureau of Census projects that by the year 2080, 17 million citizens will be 85 years old or older (*Monthly News from the U.S. Bureau of the Census and You* 24[2], Feb. 1989). The escalating population of older persons in our society is reflected by the increased number of elderly patients in hospitals, nursing homes, boarding homes, and other long-term care facilities. In fact, it has recently been estimated that of the 2.2 million persons who were 65 years old in 1990, 43 percent at some time in their remaining years will be cared for in a long-term care facility (P. Kemper and C. M. Murtaugh, *New England Journal of Medicine* 324[9]:595–600, Feb. 28, 1991).

Although many elderly persons are cared for at home by their children or other relatives, the burden of complete care in the final stage of life typically falls on caregivers and other workers in health care institutions. Those with direct care-giving responsibilities (for example, nursing assistants and physical therapy aides) must handle intense interaction with their elderly patients. For example, according to the 1990 *Statistical Abstract of the U.S.*, 90.3 percent of the nursing home population between the ages of 75 and 84 years require assistance in bathing, 75.9 percent assistance in dressing, and 60.3 percent assistance with using the toilet.

Yet, in many cases, such direct caregivers are given only a brief introduction to interpersonal communications during their training. Although training curriculums concentrate on the necessary technical skills, in actual care-giving situations, nursing assistants, physical therapy aides, nurses, and other health care workers must attend to the *whole person*, not just to a broken arm or a hearing problem or some other specific health problem or disability. Caring for the whole person requires *listening*, *understanding*, and *communicating*. Unfortunately, owing to several factors, these skills don't always come naturally for some caregivers:

- In our society, aging is often seen as a negative rather than a natural occurrence (advertisements, for example, continually promote youth as the only desirable stage of life). Therefore, many people have stereotyped ideas about the elderly and discriminate against them. Such prejudice against the elderly (in the form of subtle or blatant ridicule) is a form of *ageism*.
- The mobility of our society and changes in our life-styles during the past few decades have decreased opportunities for intergenerational living, and so some young caregivers have simply never been around the very old.
- The physical and psychosocial impairments of older persons often present difficulties not anticipated by caregivers.

It is for these reasons that we have written this book. There are books for the children of elderly persons and books about the process of aging or the complications of living and working with older persons, but few help answer this fundamental question: *How can I as a health care worker approach conversations with elderly patients or residents with more depth and skill?*

This book can be used by health care personnel at all levels who work with the elderly. The book can also be used in continuing education classes and training programs for those who work with the elderly in hospitals, nursing homes, and other health care institutions. It would also be useful to caregivers in noninstitutional settings.

The four chapters of the book can be used in training programs organized around four one-hour sessions. Each chapter addresses the interpersonal communication *problems* that caregivers might encounter and alternative *solutions* for handling the problems. The beginning of each chapter also includes a list of the skills to be learned. (A teaching outline for each chapter is provided in appendix C.) Each chapter also illustrates solutions to some specific problems by identifying the problem and indicating various alternative solutions. There are exercises throughout the book that can be completed individually or in small groups. (Model answers are provided for most of the exercises in appendix D.) Finally, references and suggestions for further reading are provided for those who want additional information on the topic.

Categorizing our aging elderly population is difficult, if not hazardous. Few synonyms for *old* carry positive connotations. We, therefore, have chosen to use the terms *elderly* and *older* and have not used labels such as *frail elderly* or *dependent aging*, although these terms are still used in health care. Throughout the book, we refer to the elderly as patients, residents, or clients.

In this book we address solutions to interpersonal communication problems health care workers encounter in *daily interactions* with elderly patients, many of whom:

- Demonstrate mild confusion or dementia
- Have some memory loss
- Have moderate hearing or sight impairment or cannot respond
- Have decreased overall physical mobility
- Are in the midst of active grief

Such elderly people experience increased dependence on caregivers as they experience cumulative losses of friends, possessions, and physical or mental health.

We do not offer technical strategies for solving the communication problems of persons with profound impairments, such as those:

- Who are in advanced stages of Alzheimer's disease or who have other advanced dementias
- Who have profound hearing or sight loss or other major communication impairments
- Who are clinically depressed

Caregivers and others who could benefit from using this book include the following:

- The nursing home activities director who routinely ends up using the same phrases with each one of the very different elderly patients—how can the director use words to approach the individual needs of each elderly patient?

- The physical therapist who looks forward to visits with an older person but wonders how to make the best use of the time they have together—how can the physical therapist improve communications to ensure that both the patient and the therapist accomplish their goals?
- The nursing assistant who seems only to be able to communicate to elderly people by talking to them as if they were children—what skills can the health care worker learn to foster more adult-to-adult communication?
- The nurse whose elderly patient seems to recall some facts but forgets others—what can the nurse say to bring the conversation into the clear present?
- The health care worker who finds it difficult to address the increasing emotional needs of some older clients— what actions or words can bring comfort?
- Every professional in the hospital or long-term care home setting who has ever thought when going to visit an elderly patient, "I never know what to say!"

One thing to keep in mind: The examples throughout the book are illustrations of the principles discussed. We recommend that you use your own words and your own style to put the concepts discussed into practice.

Developing Communication Skills

Chapter 1 provides the skills to:

1. Improve ways to open and close conversations
2. Introduce and sustain conversational topics
3. Be honestly attentive to patients' words and actions
4. Respond appropriately to various patient emotions
5. Clarify the purpose of the visit and the conversation

Introduction

Any caregiver who has ever thought, "I just don't know what to say" when talking with an elderly client probably is becoming aware of the necessity for good communication in the health care setting. For example:

> "I pride myself with being able to set my patients at ease, talking with them, listening to them in ways that really improve the care I provide," said Meg, a nursing assistant. "But sometimes Mrs. Johnson really stymies me. I don't know how to even start talking about anything other than the task I'm in her room for . . . and I know there's more to it than that. I find myself dreading going into her room because conversation just doesn't come naturally and flow easily."

Meg is asking herself, "Why is it hard for me to talk with Mrs. Johnson?" Of course, some older people in health care facilities are completely independent and lucid, and conversations with them are comfortable and normal. There are others, however, whose circumstances put the burden of conversation on the caregiver. The caregiver might find elderly people who are sometimes mildly confused or forgetful and, to complicate matters, those whose physical senses and physical mobility are decreasing. The elderly also experience many cumulative losses of those things many younger persons still have:

- Their family members and loved ones
- Their neighbors and friends
- Their independence
- Their own homes
- Their health
- Their reputations
- Their self-esteem
- Their satisfaction with life

Because they live in an institution, they can no longer participate as actively as they might wish in daily living or in outside experiences. They face threats to their independence, intrusions into their privacy, and some loss of control over their own lives. Their advanced age, altered health, and patient status are visible reminders of their losses. These visible reminders might, in turn, prompt us to feel awkward and be tempted to maintain a cheerful, chatty conversation. There is, too, the added dimension of the caregiver role, which frequently defines our conversation and limits our perceptions of the elderly as "patients only." So, we find it hard to realize that these elderly people are still fully adult persons, and we avoid getting to know who they are, what they feel, and how life is treating them.

We need to look for ways to challenge our patterns of empty conversation and ask: "How can I approach this conversation with more depth and skill?" The essential question Meg needs to ask is "How can I move beyond my awkwardness and meet Mrs. Johnson as a *person*, not an *old* person?"

If we could improve communication skills, we might see:

- A reduction of our own stress as caregivers when we understand better ways to interact and communicate
- A reduction of patient stress and frustration as they feel understood and acknowledged
- An improved level of patient cooperation with treatment and routine care

- An increased enjoyment of work as we get to know our patients as persons

To begin our work, let us think of a conversation as though it were a dialogue in a film. This dialogue has a time frame in which it exists, almost like a life span, with an opening, a continuation, and an ending.

When a conversation with an elderly person becomes difficult, you can begin to work on each of these separate parts of your dialogue — the beginning, middle, and end. Obviously, the beginning is the initiation of the conversation, and so this stage will be discussed first. This chapter will also discuss how to keep a conversation going by exploring and responding to feelings and understanding silences. Finally, the chapter will give some hints on how to conclude conversations in satisfying ways.

Initiating a Conversation

Many times as a health care worker, *you* are the one who initiates the visit to a patient, resident, or client, and so you are the one who opens the conversation. Sometimes the patient initiates a visit by asking for you, but as the one who comes to the patient's room when your schedule allows, you usually open the conversation by saying hello or by identifying yourself.

When you have prepared for the visit, you know your purpose and time limit, and you may have some expectations as to your possible reception. However, having good skills to initiate a conversation can enhance your entire visit because each encounter has never happened before — it is fresh and unique and can present new challenges.

When Brad went into Mr. Keller's room to administer his special medication, he noticed that Mr. Keller's eyes were red and that he seemed nervous. Mr. Keller was standing at first and then he just turned to stare out the window overlooking the little garden. Usually, Mr. Keller smiled when staff came into his room, and so Brad knew conversation was not going to be easy.

Identify the Problem

Brad has only about five minutes to complete his task (administering the medication), and yet Mr. Keller seems unusually upset this morning. Brad is worried that if he acknowledges Mr. Keller's mood he will find himself in a difficult emotional or time-consuming situation. How should he initiate this conversation?

Explore Alternatives

Brad has several options:

1. He can focus on the task at hand and not address Mr. Keller's changed emotional state: "Time for your morning routine, Mr. Keller."
2. He can acknowledge that Mr. Keller is upset and then change the topic: "Mr. Keller, you don't look too happy this morning. Well, anyway, the weather looks nice today. Ready for your dose?"
3. He can attend not only to his task but also to the whole person as he acknowledges Mr. Keller's situation: "Mr. Keller, your eyes are red and you seem upset this morning. What is wrong?"

Beginning a visit with an elderly resident is like taking a walk and coming to a fork in the road: one direction (options 1 and 2 above) can lead to empty chatter, and the other (option 3) can lead to a mutually satisfying conversation and an opportunity to identify a patient's problem. Of course, if Brad chooses either option 1 or 2, he may get his task done on time without entangling himself in an emotional or time-consuming conversation. But if he chooses option 3, he will be granting Mr. Keller the opportunity to have an adult-to-adult interaction and provide a chance for him to talk about what is bothering him rather than continuing to fret. Mr. Keller may or may not start talking to Brad or explaining his problem, but he will probably feel more as though he mattered to someone.

Choose a Solution

Brad chose the third alternative as the best way to start the conversation. This option required him to use three important techniques:

1. Immediately focusing on the older person's physical and emotional state

2. Giving the other person his total attention
3. Asking open-ended questions—*real* questions for which real answers are expected and which require more than an answer of yes or no

Focus on the Person's Physical and Emotional State

Focusing on and assessing the older person's physical and emotional state can actually be started before the visit. When it's not a first contact, you might begin by recalling things that happened before. Was he ill? Could he hear you? What were his spirits like? While reflecting on the past visit, you'll recall some of the atmosphere of being together with the person, and you can prepare yourself for the coming visit.

When you do get together, immediate and focused awareness on your part is important since insensitive entrances can hinder any further rapport. For example, heartily shaking an arthritic hand, not noticing a missing hearing aid, or ignoring a depressed mood could prevent the conversation from even getting started or ensure that it starts off on the wrong foot. But if you ask a few questions and make some careful observations, you can make the initial contact immediately productive. First, ask some questions that can help you understand the older person's present state, such as:

- "How has your day been going so far?"
- "Are you able to hear me when I talk like this?"
- "Is this a good place for me to sit so you can see me?"
- "When I was here Tuesday, you were having a bad time with your stomach. How are you feeling today?"

Giving this attention at the *beginning* of the conversation shows the patient that you have his or her best interest in mind.

By asking questions and listening to the responses, you can learn a great deal about how the patient's day is going by *looking* at what the person is showing:

- *How is the person sitting?* If he or she is slumped in the chair, see whether you can help. For example, you could say, "You look uncomfortable today. May I help you sit up?"

or "Would you like to have a change of scenery? I'd be glad to go for a walk with you."

- *Does his or her face register calm or disquiet, delight or pain?* If he or she has a twinkle in the eye and is sitting on the edge of the chair, you might ask: "How are you today? You seem excited about something!"
- *Does the person sit rigidly, or is he or she relaxed?* If the resident is sitting stiffly, it might be helpful to observe: "You're sitting so rigidly—it seems like you're not as relaxed as usual. Is something bothering you?"
- *Is the person's hearing aid in place and turned on?* If the patient usually hears you, but one day seems to be having difficulty following your conversation, try: "You seem to be having a hard time hearing me today. Is your hearing aid working? May I help you adjust it?" It is very frustrating to have to pretend to hear, and yet older people seldom call attention to their inability to hear.
- *Is he or she looking at you or at the television or out the window or at the floor?* If the person is usually attentive to you, but today you find him or her looking away repeatedly, ask: "You seem to be looking for someone or something. . . . (pause) Is everything okay? What are you looking for? I can do your treatment now or in an hour. Which would you prefer?" The strong sense of propriety in some older people often makes it hard for them to volunteer their preferences. It is important not to assume that they want to talk.

Being alert and looking for clues such as those observed about Mr. Keller will assist you in becoming sensitized so that you will be able to really communicate with the other person. Such awareness is necessary for you to give full and honest attention to the elderly person you are with. Exercise 1-1 can help you think of ways to begin conversations. The keys to initiating conversation are giving the older person your total attention and asking open-ended questions.

Give the Older Person Your Total Attention

The person you are visiting will sense your attention more easily if you convey interest, clarify the purpose of your time together, and structure the time to meet that purpose.

Exercise 1-1. Initiating a Conversation

Instructions: Working with a partner, think of four questions you might ask as you initiate a conversation. Remember, the key is to focus on the patient's physical and emotional state. To help, think of questions you appreciated at a time when you were ill, or think of a question you have heard a respectful doctor or nurse ask a patient at the beginning of an interview.

1. _____

2. _____

3. _____

4. _____

Convey Interest

You can immediately do certain things to help both you and the elderly person focus on each other during the visit. Remember to:

- Meet at eye level rather than stand while he's still sitting.
- When the television is on, ask whether you can turn it off, saying: "I can't hear you well with the TV on; may I turn it off?"
- Ask where the person would like to visit and go there rather than starting to visit wherever you meet. Try to find a place that respects his or her need for privacy.
- Face each other without physical barriers, such as office desks or kitchen tables.

In these first minutes together you can also set a tone that demonstrates you aren't in a hurry—that you feel welcome in his or her room. In these early moments, you can show that you are glad to be with him or her and that the person has your complete attention. This important aspect of honest attention can be communicated by *what you say* and by *what you do*. Complete exercise 1-2 on the next page to practice ways of giving respectful attention to a patient.

Clarify Purpose

People come together for numerous reasons. They come to health care professionals for advice, education, conversation, medical

Exercise 1-2. Showing Respect

Instructions: Here are two lists of possible responses to older persons. The ones on the right demonstrate positive comments and the ones on the left show disrespect. Working alone or with a partner, add another possible *positive* response in the blanks provided.

Rather than:	Try:
1. "Is that all?"	A. "Do you have any more questions about your new program?"
	B. _____
2. Standing at the foot of the bed	A. Sitting comfortably near the head the bed
	B. _____
3. Looking at your watch	A. Looking at the patient
	B. _____
4. "What do you want?"	A. "How can I help you this morning?"
	B. _____
5. "I just have a minute and I'm not even going to put my tray down."	A. "I'm really happy to see you looking so well today."
	B. _____

intervention, relief from boredom, and reassurance. Caregivers may come to a patient to supervise or administer medication, provide patient education, chat informally, give treatment, show affection, take a change of pace from other duties, or complete an assessment.

Most of us come to meetings with *more* than one goal. We serve our patients best when we share our goals. We can say:

- "I'm here to check you blood pressure, Mr. Bodin."
- "I'm here to take you down to physical therapy."
- "I want to hear how you're feeling."
- "I had a break and wanted to see you to tell you about my good news."
- "I had to get away from my paperwork and see a real person for five minutes."

You can also serve your patients well if you become aware of *their* goals, and the best way to do that, if you are unsure, is to ask:

- "Hi! Do you need me to help you walk around a bit?"
- "Is there anything else you'd like after I change your dressing?"
- "Would you like to chat for a minute?"
- "I heard you wanted to see me. What can I do for you?"

Identify the Problem

When patient and caregiver's purposes match, an uncomplicated visit usually follows. But when the patient wants someone just to listen and the caregiver wants the patient to listen to instructions, both may end up frustrated.

Explore Alternatives

When the caregiver's goal and the older person's goal for an interaction are in conflict, you could do one of the following:

1. Take all your time addressing the patient's immediate goal. This approach would mean you would not be able to give attention to your objective.
2. Take all your time addressing your objective. This method means the patient's concern would be ignored.
3. Respond briefly (but as completely as possible) to the patient's need at the beginning of the interaction, and then proceed with your care-giving task. Or attempt to address the patient's agenda at the same time you are performing a procedure.

Choose a Solution

Responding briefly to patients' needs and desires will ensure that their goals, as well as yours, will be met. For example, if the patient seems to want a listening ear and the caregiver is coming in to instruct the patient on using a walker, one minute given to listening will convey attention. If the patient wants simple affection and the caregiver wants to do an examination, a lingering handshake prior to the exam can communicate caring. Exercise 1-3 will help you to develop ways to respond under some conflicting circumstances or special situations when contact must be limited.

Exercise 1-3. Communicating in Special Situations

Instructions: With a partner, write down at least one thing you could say or do to communicate caring in the following four situations.

A. The resident wants to talk, but the caregiver is behind schedule.

_____

_____

B. The patient wants medical treatment, but the caregiver is making an assessment.

_____

_____

C. The patient needs some help that could wait, but across the hall, another patient needs assistance immediately.

_____

_____

D. The client wants to show you a letter he received, and you're already far behind your schedule.

_____

_____

Structure Time

When time for the visit is limited, it is helpful to let the older person know that at the beginning of the conversation. You might say:

- "I'm so glad to see you, but I only have five minutes to be with you before I need to care for another patient."
- "Two of my co-workers called in sick this morning and I'm sorry I have less time than usual. But we can have ten good minutes together!"
- "I am really interested in how you're doing, and so I have scheduled a half-hour to visit with you now."

This approach clarifies that the time you mention will be only for the both of you and that you will have each other's attention. It also allows the older person the opportunity to structure the time to suit his or her needs. The older person may want to catch up on news as well as tell you something important. Knowing the time limit helps the other person to accomplish both goals and avoids the disappointment of having never gotten to the point of the conversation he or she had anticipated sharing with you.

Ask Open-Ended Questions

Open-ended questions invite people to share thoughts and feelings, whereas closed questions require that they answer with just one word or a yes or no. An important way to make the most of the time you have with a patient or client is to ask an open-ended question to which you expect a *real answer.* Here are some examples of open-ended questions:

- "What has your day been like today?"
- "What different things have you been thinking about this afternoon?"
- "I haven't seen you for a week. What was your week like?"
- "You saw the doctor this morning. What did she have to say?"
- "I haven't seen you since my week off. How did my replacement do?" Or "What did my replacement do differently?"
- "Your eyes are red. What happened?"
- "I don't know you very well. What would you like to tell me about yourself?"
- "What would you like to talk about while I help you with your bath?"
- "I got your page. How may I help you?" Or "What would you like?"

Such open-ended questions help move you into full conversation. They also help reveal the thoughts, feelings, and needs of the older person.

Exploring and Responding to Feelings

As a health care worker, you are coming into contact, not just with a body or physical being that needs care, but with a body, a mind, and a spirit that are placed in your care. Most health care workers are trained, of course, to help mend the body, not the mind or the spirit; the exceptions are psychiatric caregivers and hospital chaplains. Yet, the rest of us cannot afford to ignore the emotional and spiritual aspects of our patient's lives.

Identify the Problem

When you take the time to ask open-ended questions, you must be prepared to encounter a genuine person because one of the consequences of asking people of any age *real* questions is that they will give real answers. For example, Alice came in to the diabetic clinic for a class, and Jill, the nursing assistant, asked her, "How are you doing?" Alice responded, "I'm really having a hard time right now." Jill asked an open-ended question, and she received a truthful answer that revealed Alice's emotional state. How should a caregiver respond to such a sharing of honest feelings and emotions?

Explore Alternatives

Jill has several different ways she can respond to Alice:

1. She can attempt to "make it better." "You look great, you really do. Tomorrow will be better." This approach just glosses over the distress the patient or resident has honestly expressed.
2. She can ignore the response and concentrate on the task. "Well now, you can sit over here until the nurse is ready to see you." This response totally ignores the patient's feelings.
3. She can acknowledge Alice's emotional state by simply stating what she observes. For example, she could say, "You look really down today" or "You seem discouraged." This approach lets the patient feel she has not been ignored or judged. In fact, she will know she has been listened to and may feel more willing to share her feelings.

Choose a Solution

If Jill chooses the first option, she is using a typical but unhelpful way to respond to someone who shares an unpleasant feeling.

Most of us don't enjoy pain, whether it's our own pain or the pain described by others, but a *real* answer might reflect pain. However, our first inclination—to talk the person out of the feeling—is rarely helpful. In fact, in this case, Jill's first response could well have increased Alice's distress and frustration by causing her to feel that she had no right to feel that way.

Both the first and the second response deny Alice's feelings. She is likely to perceive that her problem has been trivialized. The perception is: "You don't think this is important. I guess I can't say anything more to you."

The third choice, however, recognizes the experience, and the patient can feel that Jill cares. She feels free to express as much as she wants about how she's feeling and thereby senses a decrease in her isolation.

Unfortunately, it is not just when people are feeling bad that they may encounter this type of reaction. Even *good* news shared is frequently met with disclaimers. *We tend to pop people's balloons rather than enjoy their flight.* If you change the subject, compare a story of your own, perfunctorily say "how nice" or go "one up" on people by sharing one of our own stories that makes theirs seem small, you are ignoring their personal experience, as well as their presence.

For example, Marie was changing a dressing for Mrs. Lane, an 84-year-old patient. Mrs. Lane told Marie about a letter she had received that day. She said joyfully, "My grandson, Tom, was just accepted into medical school! I am so proud of him." Marie replied, "That's nice. You remember that my boy, Bill, is already practicing law, and my girl, Julie, is graduating from medical school in May."

The nurse missed an opportunity to enjoy Mrs. Lane's good news. She also effectively ended the conversation. Think of a better answer Marie could have given Mrs. Lane. When you choose the option of acknowledging the feelings of a patient who tells you he's having a wonderful *or* terrible day, you can use these four techniques: (1) recognize feelings, don't deny their existence; (2) stay with, rather than distract; (3) explore and invite the person to expand; and (4) look for resources and successes in past experiences.

Recognize Feelings

Examples of your responses that recognize the other person's feelings include the following:

If the older person says:	You say:
"I'm really upset today."	"You're having a hard time." Or "What's the trouble?"
"I'm so eager to see her."	"You're really excited." Or "What do you like to do with her?"
"He makes me so mad!"	"It's hard on you." Or "What happened?"
"Why doesn't she just call?"	"You're worried." Or "When did you hear from her last?"
"You won't believe my good news!"	"What is it?" Or "You really look happy!"

Now do exercise 1-4 to see whether you can recognize feelings.

Stay With Rather Than Distract

We sometimes feel that the emotions of fear, anger, unhappiness, and distress are "negative." Yet, it is helpful to remind ourselves that an emotion is neither "positive" nor "negative" but simply

Exercise 1-4. Recognizing Feelings

Instructions: With a partner, choose the role of either patient or caregiver. Have the patient speak the sentences shown on the left and the caregiver think of a response that recognizes the feelings and doesn't judge them.

Patient	Caregiver
1. "I wish I could get out of here."	
2. "He never writes to me."	
3. "I'm scared to see the doctor."	
4. "My stomach stopped hurting this morning!"	

human. And it is certainly human for a patient to have feelings such as unhappiness when circumstances have brought him or her to a long-term care facility.

However, from habit or fear of addressing a person's emotions, we frequently respond to a shared "negative" feeling with a comment that moves the conversation away from the pain. This move away is a *distraction* from the openness of spoken suffering. In other words, we try to distract the patient from the discomfort. We do this by:

- Changing the subject
- Comparing our own experience (or someone else's) with theirs
- Judging the patient's feelings
- Ignoring the patient's feelings

When we make these distractions, we are not inviting the patient to share with us — we are shutting the doors to further conversation. With a little practice, however, you can continue to communicate. The most effective method is by asking more open-ended questions.

For example, when an older person says he is really mad at his daughter:

Try:	Rather than:
"What is that like for you?"	"Have you heard from your son?" [Changes the subject]
"What happened?"	"My daughter makes me mad, too." [Makes a comparison]
"What does that mean to you?"	"It'll be better tomorrow." [Closes by ignoring feelings]
"What's wrong?"	"Shame on you. At least she visits!" [Closes by judging]

Explore and Invite the Person to Expand

Elderly people often want to say more in a conversation but want some reassurance that you're interested in what they're saying.

Interest can be conveyed by questions or comments that explore what the other person is feeling. For example, consider the man who says he's mad at his daughter. After asking him what happened, you can explore further with questions or comments such as:

- "How do you two usually get along?"
- "Have you ever had an experience like this before?"
- "How did that one work out?"
- "What is this like for you?"
- "Tell me more."
- "What does it make you feel like doing?"

This type of exploring can lead to positive results by:

1. Decreasing isolation: the older person feels someone cares.
2. Initiating a satisfying conversation: you have focused on the immediate needs of the older person, rather than on unrelated trivia.
3. Increasing intimacy and knowledge of the other: you are finding out what matters to the person you're visiting.

Being listened to and being able to express feelings helps the older person to sort out emotions and make more sense of them.

Look for Resources and Successes in Past Experiences

We all have resources within us, although at times the experience of helplessness blinds us to the strength we've found in the past. Consider Rosemary's experience: Rosemary was a retired banker who recently had a stroke, leaving her confined to a wheelchair. She was highly regarded in her community as a competent businesswoman, an involved citizen, and a caring friend. She was known as "someone who understands." Karen, the home health aide, was making the bed during the following conversation:

Rosemary: "I'm so glad you came. It's so lonely."
Karen: "Do you feel lonely?"
Rosemary: "Oh . . . ever since I can't get out and about I feel like my life is receding from all those who still go to work each day."
Karen: "Receding? That could be kind of scary. What's that like for you?"

Rosemary: "I get to feeling silly. I was just getting used to being retired, and then this came. I probably should be glad I still have my faculties, but—I'm just not used to being so confined!"

Karen: "It must be hard. You had a really busy life."

Rosemary: "I miss people most. Some days I feel like I'll starve if I don't have a decent conversation with someone outside of this house."

Karen: "When you were working, people found you a great listener. I've heard lots of your friends comment on how you could carry on a conversation on a wide variety of topics because you're so well-read. I wonder how you could get out now or where you could find people to be with?"

You can invite the older person to look for his or her own resources by asking open-ended questions about past behavior, as Karen did. Such questions can result in the older person recalling successful strategies from his or her past that might help them find a workable approach to the present situation.

Understanding Silences and Keeping a Conversation Going

A visit with no planned agenda frequently presents you with the frustrations of silences and those moments when you wonder how to sustain *any* conversation. Since words are a key way (along with touches, smiles, and so forth) to relate to another person, we sometimes feel that silence is negative. And it is true that some synonyms of silence are "dumbness," "unresponsiveness," and "uncommunicativeness." Yet, other synonyms of silence are "calm," "stillness," and "peace," which are a more positive way to view silence. How should you deal with dead-end conversations or silences?

Identify the Problem

You might have felt very comfortable initiating the conversation with an older person and then come to a dead end; your comments are not acknowledged and you are met with silence. With the elderly there could be several reasons for this happening:

- You may not have been heard.
- The other person may not want to hear.
- A common topic of interest may be lacking.
- An emotional barrier may prevent words.
- One of you may be thinking or remembering something unrelated to the conversation.
- One of you may no longer be interested in the topic being discussed.
- One of you may be thinking of the next thing to say.
- One of you may want to rest in the silence together with the other.
- The older person may be tired and his or her energy to visit may be gone.

Explore Alternatives

Our tendency in this type of situation is to attempt to fix the silence right away. It seems as long as we're "communicating" that things are normal. Also, sometimes we talk nonstop because we feel a need to control the direction of a conversation, fear what isn't being said, or feel we must eliminate silences in order to be good listeners.

The fallacy behind this is the assumption that all silences are negative. A special, warm silence may be a very normal and comfortable habit between you and the other person—a cozy silence that can be treasured. Some silences are preparatory, giving needed time for thought. If, however, it seems an atypical silence, you need to choose either to affirm the silence or to attempt to find its source.

Choose a Solution

Probably the best way to find out about some silences is simply to *describe what you see and wait for a response:*

- "You seem so much more quiet today. How is your day going?"
- "You didn't answer me, Mrs. Peters. Are you able to hear me?"

If you feel that asking about a silence is out of place, you can choose to affirm that quiet time. Here are some ways to do that:

- Stay quiet, don't interrupt with your words.
- Silently recall that some emotions can't be expressed in words.
- Accept any tears or sadness without speaking.
- In a silence of intense emotion, refrain from judging. For example, don't say in an accusing voice, "You cry every time I bring up the subject of your husband."
- Use touch (hugging, patting, or holding a hand) when appropriate.

Now do exercise 1-5 to see whether you can handle silences.

But what if your silence is only because neither of you can think of a topic to talk about? Following are some useful hints to keep the conversation going. These include using open-ended questions, nonverbal affirmations, and nonword or one-word affirmations.

Use Open-Ended Questions

Open-ended questions are the best tool to keep a conversation from flagging. They also enable you to explore what the older person is feeling. For example:

1. *Ask memory questions.* "Out of all the places you have lived, what made some better than others?" "What was your role in that little town during World War II?" "What made you change your occupation so late in life?" "You

Exercise 1-5. Understanding Silences

Instructions: Choose a partner and have one person play the role of the patient and the other the caregiver. Assume that the patient is someone who usually chats but on this visit is silent or only answers with one word or a grunt. Using the suggestions in chapter 1, create a scene that shows how the caregiver can deal positively with the patient's unusual silence. Indicate what the caregiver could say to the patient.

---

must remember what you were doing on Pearl Harbor Day. What happened? What was it like?" "When you were growing up, what concerns did parents have about their teenagers?" "Whom did you most admire when you were in your twenties?"

2. *Ask family history.* "How did your grandparents meet?" "How did people in your family spend their time?" (In politics, sports, and so forth?) "What were some of your favorite family meals? Who cooked?" "What do you remember most about your childhood on the ranch?"

3. *Inquire about recent changes in the person's life.* "What was your doctor's visit like last week?" "What is it like with your new roommate?" "How was your visit with your niece?" "How is your new therapy program going?"

4. *Ask a "wish" question.* "If you could have three wishes today, what would they be?" "When you were young, if you could have gone anywhere, where would you have gone?" "If you won a free trip anywhere in the world tomorrow, where would you go?" "If you had a magic wand, what would you wish for?"

5. *Bring up practical or factual topics.* "Tim has been asking about those cookies that were his favorites. Can you give me the recipe? Could you help me make them?" "All of your kids have such full lives. What were your guidelines for raising them?" "The church is trying to put together a history of its early years. What do you remember about that time?" "How were sick older people cared for when you were young?" Sincerely tap their wisdom and experience.

6. *Ask how and why questions.* "How did you work with so many different people and get along so well with them?" "I really have a problem with my neighbor. What would you do if you were in my shoes?" "Why did you choose engineering as a career?" "What was nursing like when you were practicing?" "You must have been one of very few women in your field. How was it for you? Why did you choose that field?"

7. *Use present events for question lead-ins.* "This winter seems so long. What was the worst winter you can remember?" "That airline disaster was so sad. What do

you remember about early aviation accidents?" "A movie is being made right outside of town — movie stars and all. Who were some of the most famous people you ever met?"

Use Nonverbal Affirmations

A large percentage of our communication is not made up of words at all, but of nonverbal messages. These silent clues can be understood as plainly as if you had said your message aloud. For example, a sincere smile when greeting a patient says, "I'm glad to see you," as clearly as those words would. Or the completion of a technical procedure with unnecessary roughness says, "I'm insensitive to your pain." Even the gift of attentive listening to the conversation of a patient says, "I care enough about you to hear your story."

To develop positive conversational skills, you need to give nonverbal clues that you really are caring and attentive. In the list below, the nonverbal clues on the left show interest and care and the ones on the right demonstrate disinterest.

Remember to:	Try not to:
Nod in agreement	Stare with no acknowledgment
Lean forward toward the other person	Sit back with arms crossed
Look into the other person's eyes frequently	Look out the window or elsewhere
Show attention with your facial expression	Look blankly at the speaker
Stand or sit near the patient during a conversation	Talk while peeking around a door or while edging out of the room

If in a face-to-face conversation, the patient can see through nonverbal clues, such as smiles and nods, that you are interested in what is being said, he or she will be encouraged to continue sharing with you.

Use Nonword or One-Word Affirmations

Besides the silent (nonverbal) affirmations of care we just discussed, you can also use nonword or one-word messages to let the older person know that you have heard and understood.

Think of a time when you had a telephone conversation with someone who listened to you in total silence. After a while didn't you feel like saying, "Are you still there?" The same thing can happen in a face-to-face conversation. If the other person does not at least respond with something like, "yes," "okay," "oh," "umm," or "really," you might feel like saying, "Hello, are you still with me?"

These little one-word affirmations ("yes," "right," "okay," and so forth) are signals that encourage interaction. They can be used spontaneously throughout the conversation to show your interest in the topic and the person. (Even laughter is a sign that you have listened carefully!)

Sometimes, however, even with all your skill, you reach a dead end. The older person consistently responds with one-word answers and seems uninterested in your visit. What then? Recognize that it might not be a good time for a visit, and give the older person the courtesy of time alone. You might ask: "Would you prefer me to come back later? Tomorrow?" Or you might complete the task in silence and leave the person alone as soon as you are finished.

Concluding a Conversation

One of the most thoughtful things you can do when coming to the end of your time with the older person is to prepare rather than surprise him or her. Announce your departure or your concluding time when you first arrive, as suggested earlier in this chapter. When it's about five minutes before the time the visit must end, alert the person you are visiting by saying, for example:

- "I have five more minutes. I wanted to tell you about my trip before I left."
- "I have two more minutes before I must report to my supervisor."
- "I have one more minute with you. Is there anything else you'd like to talk about?"
- "We have five more minutes and you haven't talked to me about why you asked me to stop by."

When the time to leave has come, leave. That communicates to the person you're visiting that you are dependable. It lets them say: "I can count on you. You mean what you say."

Parting company is one of the few times our "hands-off" society allows touch. Take advantage of this freedom to give a lingering handshake or reach out to hold hands as you say goodbye. When it's time to leave, a gentle hand on the patient's arm can give comfort and a sense of completion to a visit.

When possible, let the person know when you might return. Looking forward to a visit can add warmth to waiting.

Conclusion

Learning to respect every conversation as a unique event will help you pay special attention to an interaction's beginning and ending. And respecting the person you are talking with will give you the ability to be honestly attentive, respond in appropriate ways, and discover valuable things to talk about. (Do exercises 1-6 and 1-7.)

Exercise 1-6. Recognizing What Stops Conversations

Instructions: First, quickly review the *right* way to keep conversations going (for example, recognizing feelings, asking open-ended questions, and so forth). Now, assume the following sentences are responses given by a caregiver to a patient's complaint or observation. Explain why these comments can stunt or stop conversations.

1. "Oh, you'll get over it."
2. "You just have to make the most of it."
3. "You'll be better tomorrow."
4. "Look on the bright side."
5. "Enjoy it while you've got it—it won't last long."
6. "Is that all you're so excited about?"

1. _____

2. _____

3. _____

4. _____

5. _____

6. _____

Exercise 1-7. Relating How to Relate

Instructions: Think of conversations you have had when you felt ignored or unimportant. Write down three behaviors of the person you were talking with that showed that he or she lacked real interest in the conversation. (For example, continually looking at a watch while you talked.) Share these ideas with others.

1. _____

2. _____

3. _____

Now, think of conversations when you felt you were appreciated and listened to. Write down three behaviors the listener used to show that he or she was interested in you. (For example, looking directly at you while you talked.) Share these experiences with the others in the group.

1. _____

2. _____

3. _____

Remember, your feelings about being respected during a conversation are the same ones your patients have when talking with you.

Suggestions for Further Reading

Coppola, D., et al. Developing a sense of community: a programming approach for institutionalized elderly. *Activities, Adaptation and Aging* 14(3):17–25, 1990.

Cormier, S. L., Cormier, W. H., and Weisser, R. *Interviewing and Helping Skills for Health Professionals.* Belmont, CA: Wadsworth, 1984.

Dreher, B. B., and Alter, J. D. *International Casebook in Geriatric Communication.* Danville, IL: Interstate Printers and Publishers, 1989.

Erikson, E. H., Erikson, J. M., and Kivnick, H. Q. *Vital Involvement in Old Age.* New York City: W. W. Norton and Co., 1986.

George, L. K. The institutionalized. In *Handbook on the Aged in the United States,* E. Palmore, ed. Greenwood, CT: Greenwood Press, 1984.

Knapp, M. L. *Essentials of Nonverbal Communication.* New York City: Holt, Rinehart and Winston, 1980.

Yurick, A. G., Spier, B. E., Robb, S. S., and Ebert, J. J. *The Aged Person and the Nursing Process,* 3rd ed. New York City: Appleton and Lange, 1989.

Conveying Respect

Chapter 2 provides the skills to:

1. Recognize three obstacles to easy conversation with older people
2. Use six points to assist older persons in minimizing confusion
3. Respond to territorial behavior in an understanding and inquiring fashion
4. Discover an older person's history in order to distinguish lifelong behaviors from late-onset behaviors
5. Offer optimal control whenever possible

Introduction

Some conversations with older people lead to irritation or impatience. Such uncomfortable feelings can be used as signals that new insight about the older person needs to be sought. Satisfying conversations can result.

For example, Jake lived alone at home during the three years since his wife died. When staff from the hospital's home health care program stopped by to visit him, the conversation seemed all too familiar:

Visitor: "Hi, Jake. How are you?"
Jake: "Not very good. Of course, what do you expect?"
Visitor: "What do you mean? You're looking pretty good."
Jake: "Can't do a dang thing around here. Neighbor kids throw their balls in my yard and run in and out like they owned the place. No respect if you ask me!"

Visitor: "What else has been happening?"

Jake: "Oh, nothing. But you should have called before coming, you know. I might have been busy."

Jake's home health aides soon became frustrated by his "negative attitude," and they came to his home with less and less enthusiasm.

When we visit older persons, we may find ourselves at a loss in understanding their attitudes and behaviors. When we don't understand them, we find it hard to convey respect. If we looked beneath the surface of specific actions or words to the possible roots or causes, however, the search might lead to greater tolerance and acceptance of the other person with different ways of acting or thinking. Some of the common reasons dealing with older people may be challenging include: territoriality and space needs, confusion, inflexible life-styles, and increased dependence in spite of the desire to maintain independence. In order to communicate with an older person, it is important to learn how to identify and deal with these issues.

Identifying Territory, Space, Ownership Needs

Like animals, we humans are protective of our territory, space, and ownership—where we live, the space we occupy, and what we own and cherish. Unlike animals, however, we are also protective of our *inner selves*—our private thoughts, dreams, prayers, and feelings.

Consider those things healthy, young people might feel are worthy of protection: (1) inside: their most secret desires, private soul searchings, thoughts shared only with a trusted loved one, beliefs about God and life's purpose; (2) outside: their own bodies, clothing, furniture, gifts, homes, yards, cars, work areas, work projects, areas of responsibility ("That's MY responsibility!"), and relationships (from family to friends). Of course, the list is endless, but this partial list is an initial clue to recognizing how much people claim as their own. These things that are worthy of protection do not stop being important when a person becomes older.

It is important to note that among the list of territory and space claims, we also feel we possess things that aren't even actually ours. We might feel we own things we use at work, such as office equipment or a desk. We feel we own the space we use:

a seat in a dining room, one side of the sidewalk, the area marked by a blanket on a beach, and a place in a grocery line. We can even "own" a reputation, a job, a family, an accomplishment, or a goal.

We demonstrate our needs for territoriality, space, and ownership by claiming, caring for, and defending what we have. When dogs keep littering in the yard, we build a fence to keep them out. When our homes need repair, we fix them. When we want more privacy, we close the door to our rooms or offices. So, when someone intrudes by gossiping, by doing part of our job for us, by doing what we'd planned to do for ourselves, by claiming credit for our accomplishments (or simply by duplicating them), we may feel robbed. Jake might have been feeling that the neighbor kids were intruding into his space at a time that his sense of control had been diminished by his wife's death and by his own failing health.

Some elderly persons are adapting to new and usually unwelcome limitations that threaten their control over their territory and space. These limitations are caused by losses in numerous areas, such as in their health and physical appearance (loss of hair, diminished sight, lowered levels of energy, loss of agility), possessions (home, garden, car), inner self (curiosity, dreams for the future, hope for certain accomplishments, areas of responsibility, memory, satisfaction, self-esteem), and shared self (friends, relatives, important relationships). Because they've been limited in some areas, these older persons might be *more protective* than before of those things that remain with them.

There are several periods in elderly people's lives when we must be particularly sensitive to their needs for territory, space, and ownership (of things, time, or space). Such times include a change to a new living situation, a move to a nursing home or long-term care facility, an increased need for physical contact and care, and periods marked by expressions of paranoia.

A Change to a New Living Situation

Consider Claire's situation: Claire was unable to remain alone in her own home, and so she moved in with her daughter and began using one of the back bedrooms. The things she claimed as her own after the move were:

- Her bedroom
- The bed and other furniture in her bedroom

- Her typewriter and radio
- Her albums and pictures
- Her newspapers and magazines
- Her personal possessions
- Her privacy
- Her time

Claire found herself adjusting to:

- Unfamiliar surroundings
- Living in a home that was not hers
- Life with adult children and their children
- Unfamiliar household patterns (loud discussions and music, teenagers coming and going, new foods, noises)
- Other people's eating and sleeping schedules

Identify the Problem

Claire felt anxious and out of sorts. Adjustments to new territory and a narrowing of "her" space made her feel lost and a bit of an "outsider." She resented people touching any of her things without asking and especially disliked people coming into her room without her permission. Claire's home health aide, Susan, felt particularly unwelcome when she came for her weekly visit. She was usually greeted with a silent stare or a frown from Claire and even the question "Are you back already?"

Explore Alternatives

Naturally, Susan didn't like feeling unwanted. She usually enjoyed her work, but the days she came to care for Claire were difficult ones. She didn't know what the best solution might have been, but thought of the following possible approaches to the problem:

1. Ask for a different assignment (this would mean someone besides Susan would be assigned to care for Claire).
2. Try to get her job done quickly and get in and out of Claire's room with as little interaction as possible.
3. Talk frankly with Claire about her move to her daughter's home and ask how she could help her to adjust.
4. Tell Claire to quit being so grumpy.

5. Talk with the family about Claire instead of talking directly to Claire.

Choose a Solution

The aide talked with Claire, Claire's family, and her supervisor and chose alternative 3. She spoke frankly and directly to Claire: "You seem unhappy when I come to your room. How can I do a better job helping you? What would make it easier for you?" Claire responded: "I'm not sure. I just wish I was home. I know I need help, and you're a sweet girl. If you would knock before coming in, we'd get off to a better start. I just feel old and useless when people barge into my room without even knocking." This approach showed consideration for Claire and was a beginning step toward other ways to offer caring courtesies. When she met with Claire again, Susan used two points to show her respect:

1. She asked before doing.
   - "Claire, may I come in?"
   - "May I help you with that letter?"
   - "Would you like me to write down your questions for the doctor?"
2. She offered control.
   - "Which do you want me to do first—clean up your room or take you for your walk?"
   - "I see that some of your things are still in boxes. Are there some you'd like to unpack? I'd be glad to help."

It is usually wise to refrain from assuming that because a person is growing older he or she can no longer enjoy possessions. Possessions can give older persons who have lost some independence both comfort and a sense of security and belonging. For example, it might be a comfort to the elderly person to have the daily crossword section of the paper untampered with, and it might be reassuring to them if they could reach out and know the light is where it always is and no one has rearranged things without asking permission. One way for you to discover what is important to another person is to talk directly to them. For example:

- "You moved from such a large house to this small room. How did you decide what to take and what to leave behind?"

- "Who are these people in the photos on your table?"
- "What were some of your favorite things in your own home?"
- "Where did you spend most of your time when you were in your own home?"

A Move to a Nursing Home or Long-Term Care Facility

When a person moves into a nursing home or long-term care facility, his or her external territory is reduced even further to:

- The bed
- The nearby chair
- A roommate
- A primary caregiver ("my nurse")
- Visitors
- A space at the dining area ("my table")
- Personal belongings
- Medications (on schedule!)

Most older persons who enter a nursing home lose control over some important parts of their lives:

- *When* they eat
- *What* they eat
- *When* and *how* they leave the home
- *Who* their roommate is
- *When* they bathe
- *When* they use the bathroom
- *How* they use their time
- *Whom* they see and *when*

Many elderly in long-term care facilities also lose the freedom to use what they once used and possessed—even space and time. Many are reduced to the very core of their beings; they own fewer material things around them that can give them definition, respect, or a sense of value. Their need for the caregiver's help in nurturing their inner beings while respecting those outer spaces, territories, and possessions still owned thus increases.

It's important to give as many *choices* to patients as you can in any long-term care facility. Schedules should reflect the patients' desires, not just the nursing home staff's needs. Ask when the person likes to take a bath, what he or she wants done in case of illness, whom he or she wants to visit, and where and when that visit should occur. Exercise 2-1 will help you think of ways to offer control.

Another example of interest in personal territory is over-attention to detail. For example, nursing home resident Perry was able to sit in a wheelchair, but was unable to push it more than a few feet. He continually straightened and smoothed the blanket and bedspread as far as he could reach. No matter where he was placed, he tidied up whatever he could reach from his wheel-chair. He didn't speak unless spoken to. His family thought he was losing touch with reality, saying, "He wasn't so fussy at home." One day an aide said, "Perry, you take good care of your area. You keep things neat and clean." He replied, "At least I can do that much for myself!" The aide then asked him, "How is it for you here? What do you think about all day?" Perry then talked about his life prior to losing his health, his struggle to come to terms with his illness, and his placement in the nursing home.

Perry was left with only the territory that was within his reach, his family, and his inner strengths. Within the past five years, he had lost his home and its furnishings through an estate sale. His car, his driver's license, and the garden he'd tended so carefully for 43 years were gone as well. He had also begun to lose the sight in one eye, couldn't hear as well as he had before, and was unable to walk unaided because of a recent stroke. Yet his need to *claim and protect* what was remaining to him was

Exercise 2-1. Offering Control

Instructions: Write down one thing you could say to offer control to an older person in the following situations. You may also do this exercise with a partner and compare notes.

1. A new resident has been admitted. Two rooms are available, each already occupied by one other person, and so the new person needs to share a room with another resident.

_____

_____

2. A school choir is coming to entertain the residents. Mrs. Shields is in her room at the time the concert is to start in the cafeteria.

_____

_____

_____

not reduced. And his desire to reflect on and integrate his past and present experiences was probably deepened.

Assuming some control over the environment is one of the hallmarks of maturity. When the sphere of control contracts, as in Perry's situation, what remains in one's sphere may increase in importance. Perry's family worried at finding him so fussy, but his territory had been greatly reduced while his maturity remained intact, and so his need for exerting some control on his environment revealed itself in his constantly smoothing the blankets of the bed. He was able to keep order in some area of his life.

One of the best ways we can show respect for the person who feels he or she is losing control of the environment and losing breadth of "ownership" in his or her own life is, again, to *ask first*. When you visit a person confined to his or her room, knock first and *ask* whether you may come in. Before sitting on a bed in which someone is resting, *ask* his or her permission, "May I sit here, or would you prefer that I use the chair?"

Ask other questions as well:

- "Where's the best place for me to sit so you can see and hear me?"
- "This plant looks thirsty. Want me to water it?"
- "Your mail is here. Would you like me to read it to you?"

You demonstrate respect for older people by *offering them some control rather than assuming that they have given up all control.* For example:

- "Yesterday, I took blood from the right arm. Which arm would you prefer today?"
- "Would you like to go ahead to the dining room now or wait a bit?"
- "Would you like some help with your mail?"
- "What kind of juice would you like with your snack?"
- "Is there anything you'd like to do today?"
- "Tomorrow's the day the volunteer comes. How is she working out for you?"
- "You need to exercise your hip. Where would you like to walk this morning?"
- "What would you like to do with the time we have together today?"

- "If you get really sick, do you want to go to a hospital or stay here?"
- "In order to provide the best care for you we can, we need to know what you want. What kind of emergency care would you want? Who would be the person we would work with if you couldn't make treatment decisions for yourself?"

A good way to remember to offer control to the patient or resident is to try to put yourself in that person's shoes. Exercise 2-2 will help you imagine yourself in a patient's situation and relate to the loss of control the patient may be experiencing.

An Increased Need for Physical Contact and Care

Research, starting with that done by anthropologist E. T. Hall, has described certain acceptable space distances in our culture, from intimate to public. For example, intimate distance is defined as being from physical contact to around 18 inches away from the other person. Casual–personal distance is defined as being from 1½ feet to 4 feet.

People seem to have expectations and comfort levels within which they move themselves toward or away from others in order

---

Exercise 2-2. Relating to the Loss of Control

Instructions: Imagine that you were just told you were moving to a nursing home because you could no longer manage on your own. Supply your own responses to the following questions in the spaces provided. In groups of at least three, talk about your answers to questions 1 and 4.

1. Who would you want to tell? _____

2. What would you bring with you? _____

3. What would you say to the admitting clerk when she asked what kind of care you'd like if you had an emergency that was life-threatening? (CPR? Hospitalization? Advance directive? Contact relatives?)

   _____

   _____

4. Once you arrive at the nursing facility, you have to choose an activity for the afternoon. The choices are (1) doing crafts, (2) playing bingo, (3) attending a book club, or (4) helping in the children's day-care center next door. Your choice? _____

---

to interact comfortably and establish the correct distance. This comfort with distances and physical proximity probably doesn't change with the coming of old age, *but health or illness changes can alter the space rules.* In general, there is a need for lessening the space between the health care worker and the elderly person. To help others with walking, we need to offer an arm; to assist them in sitting more comfortably, we often physically lift them; to be heard when someone's hearing is dim, we need to stand close, facing them directly and speaking clearly.

Therefore, to show respect for the space needs of the older person, simply:

1. Ask before invading a patient's personal space.
   - "Can I help you button that?"
   - "Would you like some help getting closer to the window?"
   - "Would you like to take my arm as we go down the stairs?"
2. Focus on the person before the task.
   - "Are you able to hear me?"
   - "Am I speaking too loudly?"

When you approach a patient to perform a physical task, it is important to describe what's coming, with respect:

- "I'll help you get freshened up now."
- "I need to change your dressing now, Mrs. Lavery."
- "How is your day going?"
- "While I'm helping you with your bath, would you tell me about your early days in the valley?"
- "The doctor wants to examine you this morning. She'll need to see your incision and will probably check around it to make sure everything is healing as it should be. This would be a good time to ask her about how much you can be exercising."

Periods Marked by Expressions of Paranoia

Occasionally, some older people when they are unable to find something assume that it was taken. "Someone stole my watch!" This conclusion could be related to the insecurity some people feel when their sphere of control is diminishing. When the list of owned things gets shorter, some of the remaining items increase in importance. In addition, some people experience feelings of anxiety (threat) regarding the items remaining, so that when they "disappear," it seems as though someone has stolen them, even though they may only be temporarily lost or are just out of the person's sight.

Some people with hearing loss fight feelings of paranoia. They see you talking and yet don't hear what you're saying. When you see signs of paranoia such as withdrawal, frowning, and hints of feeling hunted or picked on, pay special attention to maintaining clear, honest communication with that person. Communicate that you care and let them know you value their company.

Your helpful response in situations like this might be:

- "You think your watch was stolen? That is really frustrating! When was the last time you saw it?"
- "May I help you look for it?"
- "It is really easy to lose things in new surroundings. I'll help you find it."

It is important not to minimize the person's distress, but also *not* to add to an accusing panic—"What a rotten place! They'll steal anything they get their hands on. Better watch out!"

Minimizing Confusion and Clarifying What's Real

Confusion is not an uncommon symptom among older people. Changes in locale, illness, and sleep loss can cause mild memory impairment and mild impairment of orientation. People may forget who is who, where they are, and what they are supposed to be doing, but they can be brought back into present reality with gentle cues and honest conversation.

Irreversible confusion is one of the symptoms of advanced dementia. Different approaches are needed for people who are confused and diagnosed with advanced Alzheimer's disease or other dementias. Numerous other sources can be found for assisting such people. Here, we will explore only tips for working with people who have reversible, mild confusion.

A common experience is that of Susan, a nursing aide. Speaking of Olaf, she said, "Sometimes I feel like giving up on talking with Olaf. He acts like he doesn't even know I'm in the same room with him. But he isn't always that way, especially if we talk about some of his old adventures or if we're talking about, say, how he did at poker last week. Yet if I ask him to describe how he's feeling today, he'll answer from a fog, saying something like, 'Are we going to go now?' "

Occasionally, some elderly patients appear not to hear or comprehend what is being said to them. Showing respect under these circumstances comes more easily when care providers remember that outward behaviors do not always mirror inner perceptions. Younger people, too, become preoccupied or distracted at times. But even people who have been unconscious recall later that almost all of their senses were functioning: at some point, they could smell, hear, feel, and taste. What observers see, however, is someone who seems disconnected from the environment. This may not be the reality of the situation.

In moments of apparent "drops" out of reality, we should speak to the older person with respect. For example, instead of talking about Olaf in his presence ("Oh, there he goes again, off in some dream land"), talk to him ("Olaf, I just asked you how you are feeling"). Touching him or her gently on the arm or hand can be an additional cue for the person to focus on the present. Instead of turning your attention away because the person seems to be gone, turn your attention toward him or her. Ask whether you might get something for him or her, gently touch his or her hand, ask what he or she is thinking about, or remind him or her that you're both *here* and you'd like to talk.

A misperception of time plagues other older people at times, and that, too, can get in the way of easy conversation. The following situation is an example.

As Mark, a physical therapy aide, related: "Clarence would seem perfectly on target most of the time, and then suddenly he would talk to me as if I were his brother. At first I felt sorry for him, so I didn't tell him about his mistake—I thought he might feel embarrassed. Then I decided to let him know I was his physical therapist."

Identify the Problem

Mark noticed a shift in attention as well as memory with Clarence. Clarence not only referred to Mark as his brother, but he seemed to be "elsewhere." At first it was awkward, and Mark went along almost as though he too were in a play of Clarence's creation. However, this approach usually exacerbates the problem for those older persons who are only mildly confused.

Mentally healthy adults value staying in the present reality. People who are temporarily confused appreciate gentle correction and assistance. For you to play into the unreality conveys disrespect to the person who is a little confused, and the pretense may add to the confusion. The person might also think no one cares whether he or she is mixed up, and he or she might feel embarrassed, unimportant, or insulted.

Explore Alternatives

Mark could have selected one of the following alternatives:

1. Pretend with Clarence by pretending to be his brother, saying "Have you heard from Mom and Dad?"
2. Withdraw from relating by not responding and getting away from Clarence as soon as the therapy task was completed.
3. Cajole Clarence by teasing him and saying, "Come on, do I look like your brother? Are you sleeping or something?"
4. Presume Clarence just got a little mixed up, and try to clarify his confusion, saying, "You're remembering your brother; I'm Mark, in physical therapy. Do I remind you of your brother? What was he like?"

Choose a Solution

Mark intuitively chose the fourth option. He wanted to be honest and treat Clarence like the adult that he was, rather than like a child.

One common reaction to elderly persons who sometimes seem to be on the very edge of reality is to treat them as though they were children. For example, "Well, I get to babysit Nancy in 302 today. She never seems to understand that I can't give her all my undivided time and attention. She follows me around and expects me to do everything for her." Some people feed into this adult–child role-playing, but that response is *not satisfying for any of the people involved.* In circumstances such as these, it is helpful to:

- Try to envision an adult-to-adult relationship between you and the older person. Then, when you are together, make an attempt to treat him or her as an adult, despite superficial behavior or temporary confusion.
- Explain clearly at the outset how much time you have or exactly what activities you can do together. For example, "Can you come to the gift shop with me? Then, I have to do some work down the hall for half an hour. I'll be back before lunch arrives."

The following points may help you to respond appropriately to an older person who seems to be slipping away from reality:

1. *Assume that the person wants to function in the present.* The person's past is a wonderful and rich heritage, but being right here and now challenges and stimulates him or her to be alive and active. For example, if an older man mistakenly said, "I wonder how Jane is today" about his deceased sister, you could help him recall that his sister died last year rather than assume that he wants to believe that she is still alive. "Jane died last spring, right around this time of year. What do you think about when you remember her? Do you have any other sisters?"

2. *Gently remind the person of what's real.* You can be honest, friendly, and genuinely helpful at the same time you bring them back to reality. For example, if Carolyn mistakenly complained, "You haven't been to see me in several months," you could say, "I was here last Thursday. Does it seem like months instead of a week? We took a walk and saw the budding plants. Come on, let's go outside again and see how they're doing. I really enjoyed our visit last week and I'm happy to be with you again."

3. *Be specific when describing people and situations.* If Marcella forgot again exactly who her grandchildren are, you could name them and give their ages, point out their pictures, or draw a family tree for her to keep handy. This approach is healthier than becoming irritated because someone is always forgetting such a seemingly simple bit of information. Or you might say, "Jerry has three kids now. The youngest must be a senior in high school—that's Jimmy. Missy is 20 and at the university. And Meg is 25 and working as a nurse at the medical center."

4. *Use remote memory (of the "olden days") to pull the person back to today.* If George said, for example, "You were born in 1927, weren't you?" you could say, "No, I was born in 1946. You might be thinking about your daughter, not me, the social worker. Where does your daughter live? How was she when you last heard from her?"

5. *Work out a calendar or chart to help the person with remembering.* Mark your own past and intended appointments or visits with the person, the facility's laundry days, doctors' visits, family visits, holidays, and so on. Caregivers can encourage families to help the older person keep up a calendar by showing how it may help represent reality for him or her.

6. *Be faithful.* When you say, "I'll be here in an hour," be there in an hour. When you say, "I'll be here next week on Wednesday," be there then. Your visit, expected by an older person, can become a connection to real time. When you are unable to keep your promise to visit, call and explain the situation.

To help you to increase your own self-understanding in working with someone who is mildly confused, do exercises 2-3 and 2-4.

Most people don't enjoy being even a little confused. It gives us a feeling of powerlessness and inadequacy, and it can be quite scary. When the confusion is intermittent, and no dementia is diagnosed, you should presume that the person wants to stay with you in the present place and time. Use gentle assists to help confused patients maintain their dignity by regaining their clarity.

Exercise 2-3. Dealing with Your Own Confusion

Instructions: Complete the following statements, and then in groups of three, share your answers to the three questions.

1. I would say that my memory is (a) great, (b) fair, (c) terrible _____

2. When someone tells me something I've heard before, my first reaction is to say,

_____

3. When I've called someone by the wrong name or when I start telling them about some plans thinking they were someone else and then realize my mistake, I usually feel

_____

_____

_____

Exercise 2-4 Dealing with Confusion

Instructions: Describe what you would say in the following situations.

1. When you go into George's room for his morning care, he calls you by the name of his wife, Marie, who died several years ago. You say:

_____

_____

2. When you see Marge in the dining room, you greet her. She looks right at you and says, "Why don't you ever come to see me? I waited all morning and you didn't come." You know you did see Marge that morning, briefly, right after she awakened. You helped her get dressed. You say:

_____

_____

_____

Looking beneath Inflexible Life-Styles

One of the behavioral traits that is occasionally found among the elderly, and one that many care providers find particularly irritating, is rigidity. Older people often have to do things in a precise, never-varying manner. For example, Gladys's choreworker could not tolerate the way Gladys prepared her breakfast. Every morning she cooked her large egg (it had to be large) in an old pan—the same one she had used for 40 years. She always used the right front burner, cooked the egg for precisely 3½ minutes, and to lift it out used the same deep spoon she had used since her husband died 20 years earlier. With habitual and calculating exactness she prepared her white toast and orange juice. Every morning was an identical twin of every other morning, and even when she could no longer cook for herself, she insisted that the choreworker continue to fix breakfast with the same precision.

The choreworker was exasperated and tried to figure out why that was. She asked Gladys questions about cooking and breakfasts and doing things the same, predictable way. "When did you start having this for breakfast? You seem to like the same thing every day. What were breakfasts like for you when you were young? You like a specific morning routine. What were your mornings like when you were young?"

She learned that Gladys had always lived a patterned, ordered life. This seemingly "rigid" old person had been a strictly ordered young person. We assume that some older people are rigid, inflexible, and unchangeable. What we see them doing might look that way, but our assumption needs to be examined. People of any age vary tremendously in flexibility. Remember that each patient has had unique life patterns—the same as you.

Do exercise 2-5 to explore your own attitudes toward change and routine.

Consider another situation: No longer able to dress herself without help, Martha consistently gave exacting instructions to the home health assistant: "I always do the left sock before the right one. No, you fold it down first. That's the dress I wear on Tuesday, not today; today's Thursday."

Identify the Problem

The nursing aide for Martha talked to her supervisor. When she described Martha's "fastidiousness," her supervisor explained how some people who are slowly losing control of what little they have left attempt to compensate by carefully maintaining control over what is left in their world.

Explore Alternatives

The aide could have used any of several approaches with Martha:

1. Say nothing and simply do whatever Martha wanted in the way she requested.

Exercise 2-5. Dealing with Rigid or Inflexible Life-Styles

Instructions: Write your own responses to the following questions. Then, in groups of three, share your answers to the questions.

1. Think about the family you grew up with. Were your parents eager to try new things?

   Yes _____ No _____

2. How did your family respond to surprises?

   _____

3. Think about your days off. Are they pretty similar or fairly different each week?

   _____

2. Ignore Martha's instructions and do the work the way the aide felt it should be done.
3. Try to get to know Martha better to understand and accept her more easily.
4. Meet her halfway by following her instructions but offering changes in the routine of her day once in a while.

Choose a Solution

The aide decided to try two approaches, number 3 and number 4. She did the following over the next few weeks:

- Admitted that some inflexibility probably doesn't hurt anyone. Even if Martha always counted her pills and said, "Yes, two green and one yellow," and took two swallows of very cold water before each pill, *she still took the medicine.*
- Surprised Martha with breaks in the routine. She invited her to participate in new activities and accompanied her when she agreed.
- Scheduled unexpected exercise or concerts and invited her to participate, accepting a no as gracefully as a yes, thereby giving Martha control.
- Talked with Martha about her current life-style and asked questions and made comments that recalled her earlier life:
  - "I have never seen anyone save so many pill cups. How long have you been saving them? How come?"
  - "What kinds of things did you save as a child?"
  - "You've cooked that same breakfast for as long as I can remember! What made you start?"

Balancing Independence and Dependence

One clear insult to many who are growing older is their loss of independence and their increasing dependence on others.

For example, Albert's daily walks around the perimeter of the grounds of the long-term care facility were his delight. One day, he fell and was unable to get up. He was outside on the ground over an hour before one of the orderlies found him.

Identify the Problem

As caring friends or caregivers, we need to recognize which aspects of an older person's life can be lived independently and which cannot. But dealing with the older person about the issue of independence can be a balancing act. Some older persons cling to the security of dependence and some cling to the security of total independence.

Explore Alternatives

Again, several options are open for responding to Albert:

1. Do nothing and hope he doesn't get hurt again.
2. Work with him to discover areas of danger and potential solutions.
3. Ignore his comments and refuse to allow him to walk outside unattended.

Choose a Solution

Alternative 2 is the most respectful of the three listed because it approaches Albert as a responsible adult. The staff caring for Albert described their fears to him, such as the possibility that he might break a hip or fall and not be found before dark. Albert realized that they didn't want him to get hurt. But he also wanted to keep taking his walks—and he did not want to be attended all the time. Together, they worked out a solution whereby Albert would alert the staff when he was going out and which way he was heading. In turn, they would set a timer to remind them to check that he had returned safely.

The key to maintaining respect is, again, to ask, remembering that often independence means control and dependence means loss of control. Here are some suggestions for balancing the two.

Assess How Much Independence Is Desired

It's important to first find out how much independence the older person wants. Observe how the person uses support systems and whom he or she depends on. Find out about his or her independence–dependence style when he or she was younger. Some people live their whole lives with fierce independence ("I can do it myself, thank you!"), but others seem unable to stand alone at all ("Wouldn't you please help me pick out the right piece here?"). Most of us are somewhere on the continuum between the two extremes.

Ask Whether They Want Help

When you are unsure about how much help is too much, ask. For example, "Would you rather get in and out of this chair by yourself? I'd be glad to help and just as glad to have you do it. Which would you prefer?"

Describe the Potential Consequences

Although you want to give an older person as much independence as possible, you must identify the potential problems that accompany too much independence. The staff working with Albert did just that. They told him that they were worried that he might fall and injure himself.

Another example is Kate. Kate was instructed to exercise to increase the strength of her legs, but she wouldn't do it. The therapist gently said, "Kate, if you choose to sit all day without exercising, you might not be able to walk by the time of your granddaughter's wedding." He spoke to Kate with genuine concern and in so doing encouraged her to rethink her earlier decision. He did *not* threaten her or belittle her. He talked to her as the adult she was.

The tone of your voice and your choice of words will make the difference between a clear description of probable consequences and a masked threat.

Affirm the Adult's Right to Make Decisions

When dealing with older people, it is important that you verify that they are adults capable of making decisions. Many times, when a frail, older person becomes dependent on others for physical assistance, he or she gives up independence in other areas. Older persons might assume, incorrectly, that if they cannot take care of themselves completely, others will "do it all," making decisions for them that they might better make themselves. We can counter this tendency by affirming the older person's ability as well as his or her right to make decisions where and when he or she is capable. For example:

- On admission, ask the patient directly whether he or she has made any advance directive to be followed in the event of a health crisis, such as a durable power of attorney for health or a living will. (See appendixes A and B.)
- When a patient asks what he or she should order from the menu, encourage him or her to look it over and order whatever he or she would like.
- When the physician asks you how the patient is in the presence of the patient, don't answer if the patient can. When he or she doesn't respond, simply turn to the patient and say, "Mr. Yen, the doctor wants you to tell him how you are."
- When a change in the patient's living situation is needed, include the older person in making all the problem assessments, plans, and decisions. Again, the guideline is for you to treat the older person as an *adult*, respecting him or her as a person.

Clarify Your Own Limits

There are times in caring for anyone when you reach your limit. It may be a limit of time ("I don't have time to sit and visit with you right now"), a limit of attention ("I've had a very stressful morning, and I can't concentrate on what you're saying right now"), an experience in your past that limits your effectiveness now ("My father died of lung disease; I don't do real well with patients who have the same illness, and so I ask my supervisor to assign me to other people whenever possible").

Knowing your own limits and conveying them to patients will add to the mutual respect that is fundamental in communicating with older persons. For example, "Gladys, I'll fix your egg exactly the way you want it, but I really would like you NOT to tell me how to do it every day. I've been fixing this same breakfast for you for months, and when you tell me how to do it I feel like you think I'm brainless. Please only tell me if I miss

45

something and when I do it wrong. Let's talk about something else while we're fixing breakfast." Or "Each time I come to see you, you want me to stay longer. I enjoy being with you. I can come every day for 10 minutes or once a week for an hour. I cannot do both. Which would you prefer?"

Conclusion

Your responses to the expressions of very human and natural needs for the territory, life-style, and independence of older people can make a difference in the fullness of their important last years. Your gentle approach in pulling mildly confused people back to reality can mean the difference between their drifting off into unclear waters or coming back into clear, present reality. The choice is yours. You can ignore their needs for control of their environment or show respect by asking before doing. You can bemoan their inflexibility or explore it with them. You can support whatever independence remains to them or add to their increasing dependence. Your choice can be easily communicated by simple actions or words.

Suggested Further Reading

Aronson, M. K., ed. *Understanding Alzheimer's Disease*. New York City: Charles Scribner's Sons, 1988.

Butler, R. *Why Survive? Being Old in America*. New York City: Harper & Row, 1975.

Curtin, S. R. *Nobody Ever Died of Old Age*. Boston: Atlantic Monthly Press, 1973.

Hall, E. T. *The Hidden Dimension*. Garden City, NY: Doubleday & Co., 1966.

Johnson, E., and Williamson, J. B. *Growing Old: The Social Problems of Aging*. New York City: Holt, Rinehart and Winston, 1980.

Kane, R. A., and Caplan, A. L., eds. *Everyday Ethics: Resolving Dilemmas in Nursing Home Life*. New York City: Springer Publishing Co., 1990.

Kane, R., and Kane, R. A. A nursing home in your future? *New England Journal of Medicine* 324(9):627–29, Feb. 28, 1991.

Magnan, M. A., and Benner, P. Listening with care. *American Journal of Nursing*, pp. 219–21, Feb. 1989.

Turning Challenges into Opportunities

Chapter 3 provides the skills to:

1. Use memories to build conversations
2. Recognize and work with your reactions to difficult situations
3. Find appropriate adult-to-adult words and behaviors
4. Talk with someone with a hearing impairment
5. Talk with someone with a visual impairment
6. Talk with someone who cannot respond

Introduction

Two predictable results of conversations with older persons that become difficult are that we simply stop talking or that we experience an increase in mutual frustration. For example, Jerry dreaded going in to provide Mr. Diaz with physical therapy each week because Mr. Diaz always repeated the same stories. Jerry would say, "Hello, Mr. Diaz. Watching the baseball game again?" "Yeah. Say, did you know I used to play semi-pro ball? I'll never forget the time we were playing in Chicago and. . . ." "Here we go again," Jerry thought and clicked off his attention and interest.

When Jerry stopped listening to Mr. Diaz's reminiscences, he lost an important communication tool. Many visits with older persons are not difficult, but there are some common communication *roadblocks*, like the one Jerry faced, that interrupt the easy flow of back-and-forth talking and listening. These road-blocks include:

- Misunderstanding of memories ("He's always living in the past")
- Inappropriate "infantalizing" statements by the younger adult to the older person ("That nurse talks to me as if I'm six years old") and "parenting" remarks by an older person to a younger adult ("She treats me like I'm fourteen instead of fifty-four")
- Lack of awareness of our own responses and reactions to the person we are visiting ("I get so sad when he talks about his situation that I just change the subject")
- Inability of the patient to speak, hear, or see well

You can make difficult visits easier simply by reversing the roadblocks: (1) by building conversation through memories, (2) by recognizing and working with your reactions to others, (3) by minimizing inappropriate parenting behaviors between older and younger adults, and (4) by learning to talk with older persons who have communication barriers.

Building Conversation through Memories

Recalling past experiences is an important part of the present for many elderly people. And reminiscences, even when repetitious, are surprising aids in shaping conversations with the elderly *if we don't misinterpret them.*

Identify the Problem

Jerry's reaction to Mr. Diaz's stories left Jerry unsatisfied. He knew that the recollections were important to Mr. Diaz, but he was very tired of hearing them. He spent his time with Mr. Diaz thinking far-away thoughts, and he wondered whether Mr. Diaz felt the communication gap between them. What could Jerry do to solve his problem?

Explore Alternatives

As a caregiver in the same situation as Jerry, you could think of different alternatives:

1. You could block out the stories and comments you have heard before, as Jerry did at first. The therapy task might get done, but the patient would receive only cursory acknowledgment that he or she is more than a medical case.
2. You might let your frustrations show in an edgy but honest outburst, "I really have heard that story too many times!" A response like this could open an angry exchange that increases rather than decreases patient and/or caregiver stress.
3. You could listen and show that you hear but not respond other than to say "yes," "I know," and so forth. This behavior might be best under circumstances where you have already tried with no success to improve your conversations with the patient.
4. You could try to think of the older person as an individual with valuable memories and experiences. Then, you might develop questions to learn more about his or her past life or present thoughts.

Choose a Solution

Jerry chose the fourth option. He decided to learn more about his patient. One day instead of mentally tuning out, he said to Mr. Diaz, "Last week you told me about that game. Tell me about how you were scouted and picked for the team in the first place." Jerry became sincerely interested in hearing this new story, and Mr. Diaz was proud to tell it. The new subject made their time together refreshing. Jerry used two important approaches to his problem: he tried to fully understand and honestly respond to the older person's memories; furthermore, he acknowledged that Mr. Diaz had some valuable memories to share—ones he clearly wanted to share with someone.

Understanding Memories

If you thought about the reasons why older people repeat some of their stories over and over again, you might recognize that the stories represent much more than merely dull repetition. Actually, an elderly person explores the life that he or she has been living while gazing into the past. Such exploring can lead to very positive experiences by (1) providing pleasant and healing

49

memories, (2) offering wisdom by sorting through life's lessons, (3) identifying patterns or themes, (4) opening a way to intimacy, and (5) resolving grief.

Providing Pleasant and Healing Memories

Memories can be healing experiences in themselves. For example, Amelia was 96 years old and limited to a wheelchair when she recounted to Tom, her social worker, the story of her wedding. As she told Tom the details of first meeting her husband, she laughed and described how they'd danced every Friday night and how they'd loved singing and playing the piano. Amelia remembered healthier times and probably boosted her own self-esteem by doing so. Although she could no longer dance or play the piano and had no one to share her days with as intimately and eagerly as she had long ago, she recalled those times with pleasure. She remembered vibrant times in her life that helped shape the person she was later in life. Feeling good as she reminisced seemed to heal some of her loneliness.

During painful, drab, or lonely times, recalling pleasant moments from the past can provide relief for older persons. It can offer a recess from the present situation and can even provide older people with the inner strength to view their current lives more creatively.

Offering Wisdom by Sorting through Life's Lessons

Reexamining the past can help people learn, no matter what their age. For example, Ted, at 86, seemed to relish talking about the numerous jobs he'd held throughout his life. He had worked the rails side-by-side with Mexican laborers, had built houses, had owned a country store, had been a postmaster, had been a ranch foreman, and had raised five children. He spoke with detail about what he had learned in each situation, describing himself as a "young whippersnapper who grew up a little with every job."

Many people as they grow older (usually starting around age 35) seize opportunities to look over their remembered lives and evaluate, analyze, and put things into perspective. As Ted talked, he was really asking himself questions that are the stuff of wisdom: "Reviewing life as I have lived it, what do I see? What have I learned? What have I yet to learn from those same experiences?

I have reached a new vantage point; is there something new to know? Who have I become? What and who have contributed to my life?"

Memories can help an elderly person figure out what life has been about and can even lead to the discovery that life has been rich, with all of its ups and downs. "What have I done?" "What has it meant?" "Where have I been?" "What did the people in my life mean to me?"

Remembering people and events throughout the years can offer the wisdom of perspective. For example, Betty was widely regarded as an optimist. At 79 years old, she looked for the positive and yet didn't deny life's difficulties. When her doctor asked her one day how she found hope, given the dismal headlines in the news day after day, Betty replied, "I just think about the really genuinely good people I've known. Wherever I've lived, whatever the decade, I have known people who are really wonderful, caring human beings. How can I not have hope?"

Identifying Patterns or Themes

Older people can also discover unifying patterns as they look at their pasts. For example, Agnes spent lots of time remembering her young-adult years. She recalled tragedies and failures along with joys and successes. She told the chaplain during a visit, "When I look carefully at all that went on during those years when I was younger, I see my husband and I weathered many a storm. We also provided lots of sunlight. We learned as we lived — and learned to expect surprises. It was a rich life together. I don't think I was aware of it before like I am now."

For Agnes, remembering was an opportunity for her to see the patterns in her life, to weave together the various threads of her experience into the fabric that was her life. She said she learned that she and her husband had approached each day with a sense of readiness, and it felt good to remember that.

On the other hand, some people who have lived their lives with habitual negative attitudes will reap only bitterness when they look over their past lives and see all that was wanting. Long-held attitudes toward life rarely change in one's last years. Yet reminiscing can still be helpful to these people and can open up new opportunities. You can ask questions focusing on the possibilities of the present. For example, "You've had a really hard life. Now that you don't have work responsibilities, what would you enjoy doing? What have you put off that you'd like to do now? With no one making demands of your time today, what do you want to do?"

Opening a Way to Intimacy

An often-overlooked function of sharing memories is *intimacy.* The older person is letting you know to whom you're talking. It is one way of saying, "I am more than what you see."

For example, when Ethel was 82 years old and living in a long-term care facility, a member of her church group started spending Wednesday mornings with her. After a few visits, Ethel started talking about years gone by. She told of raising five children alone after her husband died when she was 40. She also recounted some of her hair-raising experiences. If someone had asked her why she was talking about long-past events to someone who wasn't even part of her family, Ethel might have replied, "I wanted her to know I am more than just an old lady who doesn't get out much; I am a person with a past, and my experiences are a big part of who I am today. We might get to know each other better now."

Resolving Grief

Finally, examining memories can help people work through the suffering caused by loss. Susan was John's recreational therapist. She found it hard to talk with John after his wife died. She said John constantly talked about his wife and usually cried when he did. Susan felt awkward and didn't know how to respond.

Memories are a necessary part of healthy grief. Chapter 4 will discuss ways to encourage grieving people to look at their memories. It will also describe ways to respond sensitively when such memories are shared. Take some time to think of important memories as you do exercise 3-1.

Responding to Memories

After exploring the positive aspects of listening to reminiscences, you need to respond appropriately to the memory gift you have

Exercise 3-1. Experiencing Memory

Instructions: Working alone or in groups of three, recall a time when you shared a special memory with someone. Which of the five results of memory sharing (healing, pleasure, resolving grief, and so forth) did you experience? Next, recall a time when a patient shared memories with you. Which of the five results of memory sharing do you think your patient experienced?

_____

_____

_____

_____

_____

_____

_____

_____

_____

_____

_____

been given. Here are four ways to make the most of memory sharing:

1. *Ask exploring questions.* Examples include these: "How old were you then?" "What was your social life like?" "What did you look for in selecting a wife?" "How did you manage that situation?"

2. *Use memory as a bridge to other information.* Roger talked about his army days and his friend Sam with anyone who gave him an ear. He'd start off with, "When Sam and I were in the army . . . ." When stories are repeated, it can be more interesting (sometimes to both the teller and the listener) to ask new questions, such as "How did you decide to join the army?" "What were you like as a young man?" "What were some of your dreams or goals?" "How is your life today like the days you are talking about?" "You speak so highly of your friend Sam. Tell me about some of your other friends from those days." "What did you do after you got out of the army?"

3. *Find a cue for a question within frequently heard stories.*
George always complained about his wife's religion. One
day, instead of trying to change the subject entirely, the
nurse asked George what role religion played in his own
family as he was growing up.

4. *Practice ways to tell the person you've heard it before.*
When Sarah told Dennis, her nurse, of the big fire in
the little town she lived in 50 years ago for the fiftieth
time, Dennis said, "Oh, yes! You have told me before.
Wasn't that the time . . . ," and then he repeated the end
of the story as he'd heard it before. He then expanded
the conversation by asking, "What other emergencies
do you remember from those days?" followed by "What
were regular days like for you then? What did you do for
fun?"

Think of different ways to respond to memories as you complete exercise 3-2.

Exercise 3-2. Responding to Memory Sharing

Instructions: Here are a few general statements that might be made by patients. Write two possible responses to their memories. Explain which of the four techniques (asking an exploring question, finding a cue, and so forth) you have used and why. You may do this exercise with a
partner.

1. "Did I ever tell you that you look like my sister?" (This patient says this *every* time the
caregiver and the patient are together.)

   a. _____

   b. _____

2. "Things aren't like they used to be." (A continual lament of this patient.)

   a. _____

   b. _____

3. "I buried four husbands, you know." (A statement made frequently to anyone who will listen.)

   a. _____

   b. _____

Recognizing and Working with Your Reactions to Others

Some visits might become difficult because of *your reactions* to the older person's comments or behaviors. When you find yourself not wanting to see the person again, putting off making contact, or avoiding going into his or her room, you might look to *yourself*, rather than the patient, for a clue about the problem.

Cindy visited Al in the nursing home each Friday during her senior year of high school as a service project. For the first seven months after graduation, she kept visiting as a volunteer, missing only once in those months. But lately Cindy found she was dreading Fridays. Each week she silently hoped something would come up to give her an excuse not to go.

When Cindy talked with the volunteer coordinator, she discovered that she had become less and less comfortable while visiting with Al. She said he had been sick and weak, and even though he seemed glad to see her, he didn't say much after "hello." Cindy felt awkward with the long silences that developed between Al and herself. She said she just didn't know what to do or say and whether to stay or go.

Identify the Problem

In our culture, many of us are trained to cover up our feelings. Therefore, we are not aware of or in touch with complex emotions. To begin to understand what is happening between you and your elderly client, you might first give yourself some time to sort out and name your emotions. Each time you resist a visit with an older person, ask yourself the following questions:

1. *What am I feeling?* Frustration, anger, embarrassment, boredom? See whether there is a pattern to your feelings. Am I angry most of the time? Do I almost always feel fearful? In our example, Cindy thought about her visits over a period of weeks and decided that she was not angry, but rather that she was embarrassed and felt awkward when with Al.
2. *What is the source of these feelings?* Ask yourself some questions. Has something changed over the time I've been in contact with this person? Have I always felt this way

55

about him? Is there something I am doing differently? Is the person I'm visiting doing something differently? In our example, Cindy began to realize that her feelings had changed as Al became more ill and weak. Her visits had been more enjoyable to her when he had talked more and when they could take walks together.

3. *Who has the problem?* Am I the only one bothered? Is it my problem? Is it his problem? Is it ours? In our example, once she had identified her feelings, Cindy recognized that she was more bothered about the visits than Al was. He didn't seem to be uncomfortable. The stress appeared to be mostly her problem.

Explore Alternatives

Once you are aware of your feelings and have tentatively identified the problem, it's helpful to look at as many potential solutions as possible. These might include the same ones Cindy was faced with:

1. Describe my feelings and my sense of the problem to the person I am visiting.
2. Recognize my feelings and be quiet about them.
3. Ask some exploring questions to find out whether the bothersome behavior is part of lifelong patterns.
4. Stop visiting.
5. Ask a co-worker's opinion. (It is important, however, to be sensitive to the older person's right to confidentiality when consulting someone not directly involved in his or her care.)

Choose a Solution

In the preceding list, the only option that might not lead to improved conversation would be to stop visiting, number 4. Each of the other alternatives could lead to new information, which, if used properly, might improve future interactions. For example, an understanding of your own feelings could lead to quiet acceptance of a difficult situation. Or identifying certain lifelong behavioral patterns of a patient could lead you to be more accepting and tolerant of the present circumstances. And consulting a co-worker (with confidentiality kept in mind) could be effective.

Cindy explored all the options and decided to talk to Al about her visits. Once she realized that she was feeling awkward when she visited him, she wanted to find out how he viewed her recent visits. She asked him whether he still wanted her to come on Fridays. When he said yes, she said, "Al, when I'm here, you seem awfully quiet, and I don't know if you'd like me to stay a shorter time or stay my usual hour. What do you think?" Al told her he just didn't have much energy anymore and would love her to keep coming but to come for only half an hour. He said he would like her to read to him sometimes and other times just tell him about her day. He added that he probably wouldn't be telling her the stories about his colorful history as he had in past visits.

Al also took this opportunity to tell Cindy how much he appreciated her visits. She was the only outside visitor he had, and he found Fridays were always special because she came.

Had Cindy chosen to stop coming, she might never have found out how much those visits meant to Al, and Al's Fridays would have lost their spark for him. As it turned out, Cindy visited on Fridays until Al died, just about a year later. Today she recalls her relationship with Al as one of the most precious of that time in her life.

Using Cindy's experience as a springboard for ideas, complete exercise 3-3.

Exercise 3-3. Working with Your Reactions to Others

Instructions: Privately, think of a time you found yourself not wanting to visit a patient, resident, or client. Now, use the steps Cindy went through and see whether you can identify your feelings, the source of those feelings, and who has the problem. Writing down your thoughts here might help put them into focus. What solution did you choose, and what was the outcome? What could you have done differently? A starting point could be to first write down the name of the person. Next, write down what you wanted the visits to be like and what they were really like.

_____

_____

_____

_____

_____

_____

_____

_____

_____

_____

Minimizing Inappropriate Parenting Behaviors between Older and Younger Adults

Two patterns of interaction frequently seen between older and younger adults do more harm than good: (1) the infantilizing remarks of younger adults toward older persons, remarks that assume the older person is no longer a competent adult, and (2) the parenting remarks of older adults toward younger adults.

When Elderly Adults Are Treated as Children

Too often older people describe situations that embarrass them because the younger adults in their lives (children, visitors, nurses, physicians, aides, and others) talk to them as though they were children. This habit of not speaking as one adult to another when dealing with an elderly person is difficult to detect in ourselves because, naturally, we don't usually listen to ourselves talking. Jan, in the following situation, had to remember her own conversations to see how she treated some patients.

Identify the Problem

One day, Jan, a nursing assistant, overheard a resident talking to a visiting friend. "I dread going to the doctor. I feel offended by the nurses and the doctor. They talk to me as if my mind has gone. They speak as if I am a simpleton! Imagine! They call me 'Marie, honey,' and they say things like, 'My, sweetie, don't you look nice today?' I get so humiliated I can't say anything back!" Jan began to think of things she'd said during the week and discovered how she too had talked down to certain residents. Only yesterday she had said to Mr. Landers, "You have some company coming! We'd better get you all gussied up. Let's wear blue today, shall we?"

The result of this pattern of interaction between two adults is that the patient may feel childish or powerless. Remember, being unable to walk or eat without assistance or being unable to see or hear with clarity does not change the fact that the older person is a mature adult. Older adults generally expect to be treated as adults and to treat them otherwise leads to feelings of resentment and embarrassment.

Explore Alternatives

When you interact with patients, you might find yourself dealing with them in several ways. For example, you might:

1. Make decisions for them—decisions they *could* make themselves
2. Offer them some choices
3. Ignore their presence or opinions
4. Acknowledge their presence and elicit their opinions

Choose a Solution

The best alternatives, those that ensure that you treat patients as adults and not as children, are clearly numbers 2 and 4. First, offer as many choices for decision making as possible to the older person. As long as older persons are capable of deciding, they should be the primary person making decisions that affect their lives: health choices, living choices, food choices, and clothing choices and decisions about how they spend their time.

Complete exercise 3-4 to assist you in thinking of choices you can offer those you care for.

Of course, some elderly people can become confused in a given situation, such as deciding whether they want to have a recommended operation. In this case, rather than making a decision for them, break down the information in understandable

Exercise 3-4. Offering Choices

Instructions: Make a list of at least five choices a patient, resident, or client could be offered during your working hours. Use categories such as clothing choices, food choices, living circumstance choices, use of time, health choices, and so forth. For example, a choice could be, "Would you prefer this blue sweater today or the warmer one?" Or "Would you like to stay out here in the lobby this morning or go by the window in your room?"

1. _____

2. _____

3. _____

4. _____

5. _____

portions and assist them in making their own choices. For example, "Your doctor is recommending surgery to fix your knee. You have quite a bit of discomfort now. Would you like some relief from that pain? Would you like to try more pain medicine? It might help. You would have a few side effects from the medication. If you have the surgery, it would mean going to the hospital. You'd probably stay there for four days. Then, you'd need physical therapy three times a week for six weeks after that, and your knee would probably be free of pain at the end of that time."

Professional guidelines will help with many important patient autonomy decisions. But the basic rule to remember is that the patient *is an adult* and that the staff should speak and act in an adult fashion with him or her.

Second, try to speak *with* rather than *about* the patient. Just as you wouldn't talk with someone else about a co-worker in her presence, you shouldn't talk about the patient in the patient's presence. For example, instead of saying, "Do you think Mr. Landrey will want to stay in his room today?" to a co-worker while Mr. Landrey is present, speak with Mr. Landrey directly. Ask *him*, "Would you like to go out today, Mr. Landrey?"

In these types of situations, it sometimes seems easier for physicians, nurses, dentists, and others to speak over the older person's head and ask the *adult children* or other care provider what should be done, rather than asking the *patient* what he or she wants. Instead of saying, "Well, since you're Mr. Cannon's son, what do you want us to do?" it would be better to say, "Let me review the choices that seem to be available and help with your decision, Mr. Cannon."

When family members answer for an older relative, the caregiver can redirect the questioning in several ways:

Nurse: "Mrs. Ball, how are you doing today?"
Son: "She's okay, except for her headache."
Nurse: "Mrs. Ball, how are you?"
Son: "Really, she's doing fine except for her head."
Nurse: "And how is it from *your* perspective, Mrs. Ball?" Or "I need to hear from Mrs. Ball."

Adults are *not* children, and unless they have adopted a lifelong pattern of relating childishly to other adults ("Oh, you know best, you tell me what you think I should do"), they are offended by remarks that presume that they think or feel like children. Even more so, they are insulted when people treat them as though they weren't there or were invisible or when health professionals speak to anyone but the patient, as in the following example.

Mr. Roderio was unable to move anything but his head. Whenever two nurses or other workers came in to help him up or put him to bed, according to Mr. Roderio, they usually talked to each other and not to him. "I feel like I'm just a piece of meat they need to turn or put in a new place. They could say hello to me, but usually they just announce, 'Mr. Roderio, it's time to get you up' and then they talk about the game the night before or worse yet they complain about one of their co-workers. Only one, David, is exceptional. Whenever he's in my room, he's right with me. He talks to me like I'm still a whole person, and I can tell you, that is great!"

When Elderly Adults Parent Younger Adults

Some older adults have developed a habit of treating any younger person as a child. For example:

- "You should go home and eat some chicken soup, dear. A girl should take care of herself when she has a cold."
- "You're not wearing that uniform again, are you? I told you it's not decent — it's too short."
- "You shouldn't be working so hard, honey. Why aren't you home with your family?"

This style of interaction might work between parents and young children, but it often builds resentment between adults. You might examine your own reaction to comments like those above and think of ways to answer. You could:

- Let the older person know that you appreciate his or her concern and leave it at that
- Use humor to remind the patient that you are an adult, "When I'm 35, at my next birthday, will you still be giving me this help?"
- Listen quietly and make noncommittal comments like, "That's interesting" or "That's a good suggestion"

61

An important thing to do, however, is not to let the parenting remarks continue to arouse your anger. Try one of the suggested strategies and see what happens.

Talking with Elderly Adults Who Have Communication Barriers

The health care team in your institution undoubtedly will have established appropriate communication guidelines for elderly patients with profound impairments such as those resulting from strokes or total blindness or deafness. But there are three common communication barriers you might encounter for which you find no structured strategy: (1) the patient is unable to speak or respond, (2) the patient has a hearing impairment, or (3) the patient has a visual impairment.

In the face of such barriers, your primary responsibility is to find out from other professional staff exactly what the communication limitations of the patient are. You should get answers to questions such as: Can the patient hear but just not respond? How much can she hear? Will it help if I raise the volume of my voice? How much can the patient see? Does she need her glasses at all times? You first need to find out how extensive the impairments are and what steps are being taken to help overcome them. Once you know that there is a communication impairment and you know what the limitations of the older person are, your solutions can include some basic approaches that minimize barriers to interaction.

Talking with Older Persons Who Cannot Speak

For a variety of reasons, some older people can no longer talk, and maintaining presence and respect in these situations demands your total attention. Some people are awake and alert but have lost the ability to communicate verbally (sometimes due to a stroke), while others have lost consciousness to varying degrees (from brain injury, for example).

It's important for caregivers to recognize that the needs for affection, intimacy, and respect haven't changed for these people; only their ability to request, reciprocate, and demonstrate appreciation in these aspects of their lives has changed. Remembering the following three points can help you see the difference between treating the patient who cannot speak respectfully as a person and simply treating bodily needs: (1) assume that the person can hear, feel, taste, and smell, (2) assume that the person can understand, and (3) address the disability and work toward realistic goals.

Assume That the Person Can Hear, Feel, Taste, and Smell

Starting with the assumption that the person can hear but just can't tell you so makes it easier to initiate and sustain conversation. The conversation is very different from most because it can seem one-sided. When comments are shared and silences are offered, however, the person who cannot speak *may* experience participation within that exchange. Unless you know that the person is unable to hear, assume that his or her hearing is normal.

Examples of ways to show confidence in the patient's ability to hear include:

- "Good morning, Mrs. Pohl. It's time for your bath. I hope you enjoy the warm water. I always like feeling refreshed after a bath."
- "Mr. Wayne, your son is here to see you. I guess times like these are particularly difficult for you, when you really want to speak. Your room is tidy, and your aide freshened you up. Shall I tell your son to come in?"

There is *never* a need for talking over or condescending to the patient, resident, or client. When you do that, the person experiences humiliation and feels insulted and dehumanized. Instead, talk *to* the patient. Explain procedures and prepare for upcoming events. For example:

- "It's time to change your position, Mrs. Rye. Mark and I are here to help you. We're going to turn you over on your stomach to give your back a rest. Then, I'll give you a back rub. By the way, this new lotion smells like almonds. It's one of my favorite scents; I hope you like it."
- "Sally and I were laughing when we came in just now because I did something really embarrassing. Can you believe I left my lunch on my boss's desk? I wish you could tell me about some of your most embarrassing moments."

- "Your doctor just phoned, Mr. Moran. She will be here in a few minutes. She's going to check your awareness again this morning. Do you remember when she did that before? She'll ask you lots of questions; she'll poke lots of places; she'll watch you very closely. I'll stay here with you while she's here."

When a person is able to eat but not speak, mealtime can be a good opportunity to describe and comment on the food and use it as an introduction to reminiscing. Eating is a social activity in most cultures. You can socialize by sharing memories associated with particular foods, and you can invite the patient to think about whatever is brought to his or her mind. You can respectfully describe scents, touch sensations, and sights and still avoid treating the older person as a child.

Descriptions that *miss* the mark of respect include:

- "Oh, just smell that spaghetti. It'll be yummy in your tummy!"
- "Just three more bites and your plate will be clean." (This suggests that the patient is a child who should clean up his or her plate.)
- "Oh! Do I smell perfume on you? Are you going to a dance or something after lunch?" (When the patient could have no such plans, a comment like this is demeaning.)

Respectful descriptions sound like this:

- "Lunch today is meat loaf, asparagus, and rice. Every time I eat rice I think of Chinese food—I love it. I bet you also think of something special when you taste this rice. Meat loaf was standard fare in our house when we were growing up. It was the first food that my mother taught each of us to cook. I wonder what it reminds you of."
- "You act like this isn't too tasty for you. I hope it isn't one of your least favorite foods. Perhaps you're just not hungry. I'll offer you a couple more bites. If you don't want any more after that, I'll stop."
- "This spaghetti has a scrumptious aroma. I'm always reminded of an Italian neighbor we have when I smell spaghetti sauce. Is it a pleasant scent for you? Scents are

really powerful triggers for memory. I wonder what comes to your mind when you smell this."

The person who cannot speak usually can feel. It is often healing to put words to the feeling you think the older person is experiencing. This is one more way to say to older adults that you think of them as adults and that you care about their feelings. For example:

- "You look discouraged. I wish you could talk so all of us who visit you could know what you're experiencing. I hope we guess somewhat accurately. If I were in your shoes, I'd feel frustrated."
- "You look a little wary. This is a new procedure for you. I know you can't ask questions you might be wondering about—I'll try to explain as fully as possible. I can't stay with you but I will be the one to come back and take you home."
- "You look really sad; I see tears in your eyes. It must be so hard not to be able to talk."

It can be a wonderful thing to find out whether the patient can give you a small signal for a yes or a no (like a blink or finger pressure). A great deal can be communicated with just these two words. Sometimes people who cannot speak can write, and encouragement and help in doing this can also be very healing. Others cannot even write, and so it's even more important to do the following:

- Recognize that they have feelings.
- Try to name their feelings.
- Acknowledge gaps between your hunches and reality.
- Convey caring in whatever way you can.

Assume That the Person Can Understand

Disability at any age can lead onlookers and care providers to presume that the affected person's ability to understand is compromised. It will be helpful for you in almost all situations to assume that the older person *can and does understand* unless you have learned otherwise. This assumption reminds you to keep conversation on an adult-to-adult level. Even though the older adult cannot speak, your comments to that person must stay respectful, as though he or she could respond at any moment. Some people find it helpful to imagine themselves in the shoes of the older person, and some even say that to the person:

- "If I were in the same boat as you, no longer able to talk, I'd wonder how people would understand me. I'm fairly confident my physical needs would be taken care of, but what about my fears or anguish or delight? How could anyone know what I was feeling or what I was thinking?"
- "You're looking discouraged, but I hope you're not feeling *too* discouraged. Your rehab therapy is really progressing nicely even though it might not seem like that to you since you still can't speak."
- "Your daughter just phoned. She usually comes on Wednesday afternoons, and today's Wednesday, but she can't make it today. She asked me to tell you she had to go for a dentist's appointment. She broke a filling at a restaurant last night. She said she's sorry to miss you today, but will be here on Saturday."
- "I know you're really sick with this cancer. I'm sorry you can't talk anymore; you seem to be asleep most of the time, too. I wonder what you think about all day . . . what some of your daydreams are."

Address the Disability and Work toward Realistic Goals

To pretend that the person is just fine when she cannot speak or is unconscious is a disrespectful game. It conveys more respect to name the disability ("you cannot speak; you are unconscious now; you seem really sleepy") than to act as though it weren't there. Once the disability has been named, conversation can focus on the presumed experience of the patient and the feelings he or she might be experiencing.

Finally, health care professionals usually determine goals with each patient for regaining optimum health. Although some patients cannot talk or participate in the goal setting, they *can* be informed of the treatment goals. Involving patients in this way engages their sense of self-respect as well as their cooperation.

Talking with Older Persons Who Have Hearing Impairments

Decreased hearing is a fairly normal and natural process of aging, and, therefore, you will find many elderly people in your care who face this communication barrier. Here are a few thoughts to keep in mind as you try to talk with older adults who have hearing impairments:

- They might feel an increasing sense of isolation because they can no longer hear footsteps approaching, the words spoken by someone talking as they pass the door, and so forth.
- A feeling of depression might also accompany hearing loss because the person feels cut off from normal interactions or even familiar sounds such as rain on the window or paper rustling.
- They might avoid social events where they cannot participate fully, or they might doze frequently.
- Because they cannot hear everything that is said, they might misinterpret conversations or have feelings of mistrust about what was said.

Here are some useful solutions to put into practice when you try to communicate with a hearing-impaired older person:

1. Make sure that there are no outside noises (like radio or television) to interfere with the conversation.
2. Face the light so that the person can see your face. Sometimes it is helpful when they can see your lips and your face as you talk.
3. Don't intensify your volume close to the person's ear. Your voice could just sound distorted closer up.
4. Make sure the patient has a hearing aid in if it is needed.
5. Speak with a loud, intense, low-pitched voice rather than with a high-pitched voice. (Frequently, patients have high-tone hearing loss.)
6. Use short sentences.
7. If you must repeat something, rephrase the sentence when possible rather than saying the same words.
8. Speak slowly, but don't exaggerate your lip movements. (It is possible the patient is helped by normal lip reading.)

9. Don't speak with a pencil, gum, cigarette, food, or other objects in your mouth.
10. Sit three to six feet away from the patient.
11. Try not to startle the patient. Remember that he or she might not hear you coming.
12. Use note writing when necessary.

Do exercise 3-5 to see whether you can identify with the frustration of hearing-impaired persons.

Talking with Older Persons Who Have Visual Impairments

People who have visual impairments have barriers to communication because they cannot read the many nonverbal cues we give along with our verbal messages. For example, they might not see a hand signal, read a facial expression, or notice a body gesture. To help in communicating with these patients, it is good to remember:

- They might be more dependent on others to help them.
- Like the hearing impaired, they might feel isolated because they cannot participate in life as they once did.
- They might feel more fear and anxiety as their control becomes more limited and they become more dependent on others.

Exercise 3-5. Working with an Older Person with Impaired Hearing

Instructions: You need to do this exercise with a partner. Have one person stand 15 to 20 feet away from you. Put your hands firmly over your ears to mute sounds. Have the distant person give you some simple instructions or ask a question. If you can hear clearly, put on a radio for background interference or have the person speak more softly. Can you understand the problems of the hearing impaired? Describe what you felt.

_____

_____

_____

_____

_____

_____

Here are some suggestions to help when you are communicating with the visually impaired:

1. Make sure the person who requires glasses has them on and that they are clean.
2. Stand closer to talk if the person can see better when things are closer. Also, you might need to stand in the person's direct line of vision.
3. Stand in the light so that the person can see you.
4. Don't surprise or startle the person. For example, knock before entering the room, and announce yourself. Avoid a sudden touch when the person doesn't know that you are there.
5. Use large writing (with name tags or calendars) when the person has some vision.

Now do exercise 3-6.

Conclusion

You can make difficult or awkward visits with elderly people easier by thinking about those visits, identifying the sources of difficulty, and choosing a response that fits you and makes your communication with them more effective and enjoyable.

Exercise 3-6. Working with the Visually Impaired

Instructions: With a partner, do the following exercise to help you understand the world of the visually impaired. Sit facing a partner with a desk between you. Close your eyes so that you can see only vague shapes and colors through your eyelashes. Have your partner put three things in front of you (for example, a pencil, a cup, and a piece of paper). Without touching the items, try to tell what they are and where they are in relation to each other. What happens to your confidence? Are you awkward or embarrassed, confident or frustrated? Write down your thoughts.

_____

_____

_____

_____

_____

_____

_____

When you see memories as possibilities for healing, for making life more complete, or for making more sense out of life, you can see the older person who reminisces in a new light. You can effectively use questions to help the patient explore rather than merely repeat those memories.

When something uncomfortable happens during a visit, you can examine yourself and any changed behavior and usually discover what is troublesome. You then can plan what to do about the discomfort, and it probably won't get in the way of the visit. When adult caregivers and patients forget to treat each other as adults, you can find ways to remind yourself and your older patients to do so.

You can understand communication barriers and work to make conversations easier. Make most difficult visits more comfortable by looking at them with honesty and gentleness and by responding appropriately.

Now do exercise 3-7.

Exercise 3-7. Acknowledging Presence

Instructions: First, sit in a group of three. Have two people say hello to the third person and then proceed to carry on a conversation with each other while completely ignoring person number three. The two talking people should even avoid eye contact with the ignored one. Take turns being ignored, and then examine your reactions. Have each person describe his or her reactions below. Remember your own reactions to "becoming invisible" when you deal with the elderly people in your care.

Person 1 _____

_____

Person 2 _____

_____

Person 3 _____

_____

_____

Suggestions for Further Reading

Allen, M. N. The meaning of visual impairment to visually impaired adults. *Journal of Advanced Nursing* 14(8):640–46, August 1989.

Beauchamp, T. L., and Childress, J. F. *Principles of Biomedical Ethics*, 3rd ed. New York City: Oxford University Press, 1989.

Carbany, L. J. "What did you say?" Caring for the patient who has a hearing impairment. *Journal of Practical Nursing* 38(3):36–39, September 1988.

Green, R. A life systems approach to understanding parent-child relationships in aging families. *Journal of Psychotherapy and the Family* 5(1/2):57–69, 1989.

Klinzing, D., and Klinzing, D. *Communication for Allied Health Professionals*. Dubuque, IA: William C. Brown, 1985.

Krach, P. Filial responsibility and financial strain: the impact on farm families. *Journal of Gerontological Nursing* 16(7):38–41, July 1990.

Lewis, C. B. *Aging: The Health Care Challenge. An Interdisciplinary Approach to Assessment and Rehabilitative Management of the Elderly.* Philadelphia: F. M. Davis, 1985.

Lichtenberg, P. A. Reducing excess disabilities in geropsychiatric inpatients: a focus on behavioral problems. *Clinical Gerontologist* 9(3/4):65–76, 1990.

Norris, R. Commonsense tips for working with blind patients. *American Journal of Nursing* 89(3):360–61, 1989.

President's Commission for the Study of Ethical Problems in Medicine and Biomedical and Behavioral Research. *Deciding to Forego Life-Sustaining Treatment.* Washington, DC: U.S. Government Printing Office, 1983.

Exploring Meaning and Purpose in Living

Chapter 4 provides the skills to:

1. Recognize the phases of normal grieving
2. Respond to a grieving person in a way that facilitates healing
3. Ask questions that assist the person in finding life's meaning
4. Respond helpfully to questions about life's meaning
5. Provide support to persons who are hurting

Introduction

Living longer provides opportunity to think about all the loved ones one has outlived, to wonder about the reason for living, and to see how suffering fits into life. Some older people outlive all of the people they were close to, and most outlive some of their friends and relatives. Grieving comes naturally at those times, and sensitive responses by family, friends, and caregivers can help an older person in healthy grieving.

As people see their loved ones die and think about their own lives waning, many look at the question of suffering and life's meaning. As patients find themselves exploring their own spirituality, the health care staff can be of great assistance. This chapter examines grief and identifies ways to recognize this natural response to loss that convey respect to the person who is grieving. Further, it explores ways to discuss spirituality with elderly persons.

Recognizing and Respecting Grief

Grief is a human response to the loss of someone or something significant. Older people may have lost loved ones, familiar surroundings, meaningful activities, physical independence, self-esteem, and even their memories. No matter how many losses someone has had, each new one is a unique experience, and each loss hurts.

A common mistake made with older persons is assuming that they've hurt worse in their lives and that this pain can't be all that bad. When others make this assumption, elderly persons are left with a sense of being totally misunderstood.

Identify the Problem

John was the nurse caring for Anna, and he was puzzled by her grief. Anna had been in the nursing home several months, and she found a weekly highlight in her friend Marge's visits. Anna and Marge had been neighbors and friends for 46 years. They had each been widowed and found solace in their friendship through their separate griefs. Then Marge died, and even two months later Anna found herself very uninterested in life. She said she felt "sad to the bone" and wondered why she kept on living. Whenever John was on duty, he tried to cheer Anna up, but he noticed it wasn't having any effect on her mood.

Troubled by Anna's continued sadness, John thought about the losses Anna had suffered and realized that Marge's role in Anna's life had probably been very significant. The deep sadness was likely the mourning of this good friend's death.

Explore Alternatives

John thought of several ways he might respond to Anna:

1. He could talk about cheerful topics, trying to get Anna's mind off of her pain. For example, "Your blood pressure's down today. I think you'll enjoy the concert planned for this afternoon."
2. He could be silent and go about doing whatever nursing task he needed to do with her and then leave the room.
3. He could meet her as a person with feelings and ask her questions about her sadness and her friend Marge. "You

and Marge were friends for so long. What do you miss most about her?"

Choose a Solution

After talking with colleagues, John decided to try solution 3. He asked Anna questions about Marge and about her having lost so much over the years, and soon he and Anna developed a special bond. Knowing more about her, he found it easier to care for her.

To be sensitive to the person who is grieving, you should ask questions and listen to the responses, be aware of the phases of normal grieving, and be sensitive to the needs of the older person.

Ask Questions and Listen to the Responses

When you talk to and listen to a person who is hurting because of a loss, it is not very different from when you use good conversational skills at any other time. But too often conversational skills are overlooked. Grieving people say that their caregivers and loved ones simply ignore their losses, and caregivers say that they just don't know how to talk with the bereaved.

The chief distinction between a person who is grieving and one who is not grieving is that the person in acute grief has little interest in any other topic. The pain resulting from the loss crowds out interest in anything else. Listening in this situation can be improved by following six easy tips:

1. *Ask open-ended, direct questions.*
   - "How did Marge die?"
   - "What was it like the last time you saw her?"
   - "What's it like for you now?"
2. *Pay attention, both verbally and nonverbally.*
   - Stay with the subject the person talks about.
   - Look at the person when the two of you talk.
   - Sit comfortably without your arms crossed.
   - Sit calmly, without fidgeting, looking at your watch, and so forth.
3. *Accept the response without judging.*
   - Using the example of Anna and Marge, try saying to Anna, "It's hard, isn't it?" rather than "That's no way to talk. We don't want you to die yet!"

4. *Explore rather than explain.*
   - Anna told John, "I'm no good anymore, and nothing else is either." John responded, "It's really hard for you, isn't it, since Marge died." He paused then, giving time for quiet reflection. When Anna didn't say anything, John asked, "What did you find helpful in the past when you had hard times and were hurting like this?"
5. *Be honest rather than hedge or avoid grief.*
   - When faced with someone who is hurting because of grief, we often feel awkward and don't know what to say. A good rule of thumb is to simply be honest.
     - "I wish I could say something to make it better."
     - "I just don't know what to say."
     - "It's hard to understand, isn't it? As you say, you've been sick for so long and Marge was so healthy and still living alone."
     - "I can't think of what to say to you."
     - "I want to be with you but don't know how."
     - "I can't tell whether you want company or not. What would you prefer? I can come tomorrow if that's a better time."
6. *Recognize uniqueness.*
   - Although making comparisons or jumping to conclusions is frequently the first response when visiting someone who is grieving, it is rarely helpful. This person has never lost *this particular* person or thing before; therefore, the grief is unique. To share a tale from your own past ("Oh, I've had lots of patients who lost their good friends—you'll get better") pulls the person away from his or her own private pain and tends to say that his or her grief isn't all that important. Your comparisons can lead to feelings of guilt on the part of the grieving person because he or she cannot respond to your concern or history as much as he or she would want to in better times. A better response would be "Anna, you and Marge were friends since before I was born. How rare it is to have a lifelong friend. I can't imagine what it's like for you without her."

Practice ways to respond sensitively to a grieving person by completing exercise 4-1.

Exercise 4-1. Exploring Grief

Instructions: Write your responses to the following questions. Then, in groups of three or four, share your answers. Have one person listen as though she or he were the patient and tell how the response felt.

1. The patient was told that the chemotherapy had not been as effective as hoped, and she is very discouraged. You come into her room and ask the following open-ended question:

---

2. The patient says, "I could have saved the doctor the trouble of running the tests. I knew the treatment wasn't working." What do you say to explore her feelings further?

---

3. You come across one of your favorite patients, and he is crying. You feel awkward and don't know why he's crying or what you should say or do. What do you do?

Be Aware of the Phases of Normal Grieving

Colin Murray Parkes described grief as a necessary and very normal response to loss. And although each person experiences each loss uniquely, the process of grieving has some recognizable, though not universal, patterns. Many grieving persons experience the following phases in the process:

- Anticipatory: preceding expected loss
- Immediate: right after the loss
- Emotion-laden: when the reality of the loss hits and wrenching emotions are felt
- Disorganization: when withdrawal is needed to experience and mourn the loss
- Reintegration: when the survivor gradually sees himself or herself as capable of finding meaning again and loving and growing again

Each phase has identifying behaviors, and each can be responded to specifically.

Anticipatory Grief

Anticipatory grief is the experience one has when loss is predicted, such as in Margaret's case. Margaret's husband Donald died recently after a long illness. Margaret recalled that she felt she was on a roller coaster during the 11 months from her husband's cancer diagnosis to his death. She said at first she didn't believe in the diagnosing doctor's competence, and so she took Donald to doctors all over the West Coast, trying to find one who would provide a better diagnosis. When that proved fruitless, Margaret was furious, saying that she felt cheated—her husband had always been a good man and now to come to this! It wasn't fair! For a while, she recalled, she was so sad, so deep-down sad, that she just pushed through each day, doing the minimum to care for Donald, to care for herself—wishing the end would come. But the last months were okay. She spent lots of quiet and peaceful time with Donald, and they talked about living and dying, and much more. It was a good dying, she said.

Margaret's experience with her husband's last months is a good example of what many recount. Elisabeth Kubler-Ross described in her book *On Death and Dying* the emotional responses to impending loss. She found people seemed to go through stages and named them: shock and denial, rage and anger, bargaining, depression, and acceptance. The stages are not distinct, consecutive, once-only boxes to climb through. Rather, they are more fluid; most people move from one to another and back again, off and on during the time preceding the loss. Not everyone experiences all five of the stages, but most people find themselves in one or more during their grieving. These labels (denial, anger, acceptance, and so forth) can be damaging when they are used to *categorize* the person grieving; they can put him or her in a box, so to speak. However, they can be helpful to you, the caregiver, in recalling what the person might be experiencing, and thus they can help you to respond with sensitivity.

The principle to consider when visiting persons anticipating a loss is to accept people where they are:

If they say:	We respond:
"Mary should switch doctors. The one that said she has cancer is no good." [denial]	"You want the best for her; I don't blame you . . . ."

If they say:	We respond:
"It's not fair! Mary is a saint! There's no one could be a better friend! Why would God do this?" [anger]	"It isn't fair, is it? That's one of the hardest questions in life!"
"No, I don't want any visitors. It's all I can do to get through the day." [withdrawal]	"It's really hard on you now. I'll tell your company to come back in a couple of days."
"I'm the one in the nursing home. If only God would take me, he could let Mary get well and stay around for her kids." [bargaining]	"Life's unfair, isn't it? You're awfully generous. You must really love her."
"Mary and I were really fortunate to have been friends for so long. I don't know what it will be like without her. I hope her last days are peaceful." [acceptance]	"What do you think about most? What's it like for you?"

Immediate Grief

Immediate grief is that which happens just as the loss occurs. The initial response to a death or other significant loss is shock and dazedness. It is variously described as "I feel like I'm in a fog," "It's as though I am looking and hearing through water," "I know I'm here but I feel numb," or "Yes, I heard you, but I don't feel anything." The need of the person at that time is to talk about the loss. So the most helpful thing a caregiver can do is ask questions, listen, and be present. Questions you can ask that lead to healing are:

- "What happened?"
- "How did she die?"
- "What was it like?"

Due to the dazed, foggy feeling many people have, your use of touch is more important than ever. One woman reported that when her husband died, she felt as though she, too, had died until people touched her, hugged her, and held her hand as they asked questions and said comforting things. She recalled the touching as being most significant to her: "I knew when someone touched me that I was here, not dead, and that I was not alone."

Simple decisions are difficult for some people during this immediate phase. At this point, it can be most helpful for you to be directive with the survivor. Say things like:

- "It's time to eat. Sit down, here is your dinner."
- "You need to sleep. Your bed is ready. . . . Come get your nightclothes on."

This period of immediate grief is one of the rare times it is helpful to be directive, telling the person what to do. Most other times, if you tell another adult what to do, it is experienced as bossy or demeaning. They feel as though they are being treated as children.

The Emotion-Laden Time

The emotion-laden time occurs after the immediate phase. During this phase, people tend to sob, cry, express anger (slamming doors, yelling, saying it wasn't fair for the other person to die first, and so forth), laugh at funny memories and cry in the next breath. The pangs of grief reach their peak, and survivors can feel overwhelmed. They are preoccupied with the deceased. Nothing else interests them. The need at this time is to talk, to be heard, and to be helped with daily tasks. It's helpful to ask questions, listen, and help where you see need.

Questions might be:

- "How are you doing?"
- "What's it like now for you?"
- "What are you remembering?"

Help will take many forms, from making phone calls, to answering letters, to simply just being there, being with the person who is hurting deeply. One of the most obvious gestures is to attend the funeral. People are surprised and very grateful to see caregivers there. They also report deep gratitude to nurses, doctors, and others who phone several days or weeks after the death just to check on the survivors.

Disorganization

Usually by the second week after a loss (after the funeral, after relatives have returned to their own homes), a time of disorganization begins. For example, Lenny didn't want to do anything anymore. He didn't go to church services, and he had always been one of the first ones in the room before. He didn't play cards or even join the others for meals. He seemed content to just sit the day away. Lack of initiative and a decrease in socialization are two of the hallmarks of this time of grieving. Lenny didn't have what it took to leave his room just to be with someone else.

Other symptoms of disorganization are an increase in bodily complaints: lack of sleep, tight throat, tight chest, stomachache, inability to eat ("Food just tastes like sand!"), shortness of breath, lack of energy, and muscle weakness. Two common signs of this period that frighten some people as they experience them are increased preoccupation with the person who died and hopeless feelings (for example, they might say something like "Why bother"; "What good is living now"; "There's no longer a reason to get up in the morning").

You can be helpful during this period by initiating contact and providing reassurance. When deep grief is being lived through, it's not uncommon for survivors to feel as though they're losing their mind, their connection with reality. You can offer reassurance with comments like:

- "You will cope."
- "You aren't crazy—it's just a really intense time you're in."
- "It is kind of frightening to have such vivid dreams of Marge as well as your husband Jake. That's not uncommon, you know. . . ."
- "Life does look bleak to you right now. It will get a little better."

Reintegration

After a period of disorganization, the person begins to pick up life again and enters the final phase of grieving, reintegration.

This happens only after the person has let go of the deceased and accepted the loss. Acceptance doesn't mean that one likes what has happened but that one is able to acknowledge what has happened: "I am here, and my life will go on." During this period, the person's initiative returns and he or she can reach out to other people.

You can help by affirming the person's progress and remembering the deceased or life as it was before the loss. Talking about the person who has died and recalling experiences that happened before the loss say to the person grieving that you, too, care and that you, too, remember.

Be Sensitive to the Needs of the Older Person

The needs of older persons in grief are sometimes overlooked simply because the people are old. We hear insensitive comments such as:

- "Oh, she expected it, her friend had been sick so long. She's probably relieved."
- "This is nothing — did you know she lost one of her sons a few years ago?"
- "She's really being childish since she lost her friend. She's been through a lot harder times."

But, no matter what the age or experience, *grief hurts*, and to assist in the healing, we need to *recognize the pain* and not minimize it. This loss has not occurred before. Many grieving people feel inadequate ("I don't know why this is so hard this time, I don't know what I should be doing"). They need reassurance to know that they are not losing their minds, that grief is normal (when it is), and that the intensity of it will come to an end. And they need acceptance: they shouldn't feel as though they are being judged on how they are approaching their mourning.

These descriptions of the phases of grief don't change when the loss is something other than the life of a person. Grief is the natural response to the loss of anything or anyone significant. The thing lost might be an elderly person's ability to walk, to drive, or to live independently; it might a loss of hearing, of memory, or of purpose. Whenever someone loses something significant, grief is the expected and usual response. Some older people have lost all of the people they had confided in throughout their lives. Some find the fact that they have so many losses at once overwhelming. Your sensitive responses are all the more important because you might be the only one they have who can share their pain and their concerns. Your assistance may be the bridge they need to find healing. Now do exercises 4-2 and 4-3.

Distinguishing Depression from Normal Grieving

Deep sadness is a normal part of uncomplicated grief. But sometimes people become *clinically depressed.* There is a high incidence of undiagnosed depression in nursing home patients, and so your sensitivity to the signs of clinical depression can be the cue for obtaining a mental health assessment of the patient.

Exercise 4-2. Dealing with Loss

Instructions: Choose a partner and have one of you play the role of the patient and one play the role of the caregiver in the following scene: Sam is 86 years old. He had a stroke two months ago and is unable to walk. He goes to physical therapy every day, but it's a struggle to get him there.

Nurse: "Sam, it's time to go to physical therapy."

Sam: "How many times do I have to tell you, I don't want to go. It's no use. And I'm of no use anymore. Why don't you just leave me alone?"

Continue the conversation; try to imagine and talk out how you would talk if you were Sam and the nurse.

_____

_____

_____

_____

_____

_____

_____

_____

_____

Exercise 4-3. Reflecting about Dying

Instructions: Answer the following multiple-choice questions.

1. My first experience with death was the death of a:
   a. grandparent
   b. pet
   c. friend
   d. parent
   e. other _____

2. In my family when I was growing up, talk about death was:
   a. common
   b. infrequent and uncomfortable
   c. very rare, if at all
   d. definitely off-limits

3. When I lose something or someone important to me, I need to:
   a. be alone
   b. have someone who cares for me stay close with me
   c. talk to friends
   d. do some hard physical work
   e. cry

4. If my physician knew that I had a terminal disease, I:
   a. would want to be told
   b. would not want to be told

5. The worst part about dying for me would be to:
   a. no longer be anywhere
   b. no longer be able to care for my family
   c. cause pain for my family
   d. die with pain
   e. have my dying prolonged with machinery or technology
   f. not know what was after death

6. If someone close to me was sick and probably dying and wanted to talk to me about dying, I would:
   a. be honored
   b. feel embarrassed
   c. feel inadequate
   d. feel I should change the subject

7. If I could choose the kind of old age I'd like to have, it would be

   _____

   _____

8. If I could choose the kind of death I'd like to have, it would be

   _____

   _____

Clinical depression will strike you as excessive grief. The person may not sleep or may sleep too much; he or she may not eat; he or she may be preoccupied with a sense of worthlessness; he or she may move very slowly or be unable to do the things he or she usually does during the day. The older person may be unable to concentrate or may show very little interest in anything. In addition, he or she may have persistent thoughts of suicide. Any combination of these signs should be a cue to seek a mental health assessment to determine whether the patient is suffering from a treatable condition.

If the person had a recent loss and you are confident that he or she is experiencing grief, one of the healthy signs to look for is that the person is moving through the phases of the grieving process. If the person seems stuck or seems to be feeling persistently worse and not able to function during the day, he or she might be depressed and would need different intervention than that needed for normal grieving.

Acknowledging Spirituality and Understanding Suffering

Losing a loved one through death or losing some bodily function through disease can bring questions about life's meaning and the place of suffering. When looking for strength in meeting the challenges of life, elderly people turn to those areas of value and sources of power they have put trust in throughout their lives. It is here that they seek meaning.

Spirituality is that aspect of a person's living that makes sense out of confusion or interprets *meaning* from daily living. It is the process of living what one believes, living one's faith. For some, faith is contained within their religious practices and beliefs. For others, faith has a different focus such as "the mark I've left for posterity" or "my family is all there is" or "work is how I've lived my life and it's how I'll die" or "what others think of me" or "my social status." For some, it's money ("the real measure of a man is his bank account"), or it can be summed up in the Golden Rule ("what I've done for others is all that matters"). Whatever its source, spirituality is found in everyone who is capable of reflecting on life.

When elderly people start asking questions about purpose and meaning and "what's it all about," when they start asking questions for which there are no answers, they are inviting you to meet them at this spiritual level of life. You can do this by quietly listening to their questioning and wondering. You can delve deeper by asking questions to explore spirituality. You can also try to respond to the spiritual needs of the person who is suffering.

Ask Questions to Explore Spirituality

Certain questions you ask can be immensely helpful to the person who is looking for answers to new questions or problems in life, such as the death of a loved one or incapacitation by a stroke. For example:

- "When you're discouraged and feeling despondent, what keeps you going?"
- "Where have you found strength in the past?"
- "Where have you found hope in the past?"
- "Who have you looked up to? Who inspires you?"
- "What does dying mean to you?"
- "What does suffering mean to you?"
- "With whom do you share your innermost dreams, your hopes for yourself as well as for your loved ones?"
- "How does this experience fit into your picture of life?"
- "What have you done in the past when you've lost someone or something important?"
- "Where have you found help?"
- "What do you think the message in this is for you?"

One's spirituality is a very private area, not openly shared with many. Yet, questions that raise the issue, such as those just listed, can be very helpful to the elderly person who is probably thinking about these very things. For you to insist on receiving direct answers isn't helpful, but to inquire, to raise the questions, can be.

Sometimes people become overwhelmed by tragedy or powerlessness. They may speak very little and show no feelings. At these times, it is useful to apply the *third-person comment:*

- "Lots of people who have lost their ability to walk, like you, at first have a hard time figuring out what their lives are worth. What's it like for you?"

- "Some people who have had so many deaths in their family, as you have, feel someone's persecuting them. What are you feeling?"
- "Some people who have lived for their work, like you have, have a really hard time when they can't work any more. What is it like for you?"
- "Some people, when they're as old as you, start wondering about what happens after this life. What do you think about?"
- "Lots of older people whose children die before them, like yours did, think God is really unfair. Where do you think God is in all of this?"

The advantage of commenting about others, in a generic fashion, and then asking a question is distance. The person has several options:

- "No, that doesn't fit me at all."
- "Yes, that's close to what I'm feeling, but I don't want to talk about it with you."
- "Yes, that's close to what I'm feeling. Let me tell you about it."
- "No, that isn't it with me, but let me tell you how I see it."

Respond to the Spiritual Needs of Persons Who Are Suffering

Ways we respond to people who are grappling with their own suffering can often make the difference between their giving in and being victims of their situations or their actively living it and remaining in control of their lives to the extent that is possible. Consider the situation with Sidney.

Sidney was 86 years old. He had a stroke two months earlier and was still unable to walk. He went to physical therapy every day, but it was a struggle to get him there. Judy, his therapy aide, felt awful every time she approached his room, knowing that he'd say again, "I don't need therapy; I don't want therapy. How many times have I told you? It's just no use. And I'm no use anymore, either. I've outlived my time. Why don't you leave me alone?"

Identify the Problem

Judy realized that Sidney might be wondering what life was about after all since things weren't working out as he'd expected them to. She recognized his distress as a signal of his search for meaning, and she wanted above all not to get in his way. She didn't want to add to his struggle; rather, she hoped she could be of some assistance.

Explore Alternatives

Judy could have done any of several things:

1. She could have offered a pat response: "God knows best," "You'll make the most of it," "Anything worth getting is worth working for."
2. She could have argued with Sidney, trying to talk him into going to therapy by scolding him: "Sidney, you don't know what's good for you," "Sidney, you're just being lazy," "Sidney, all you ever do is complain."
3. She could have asked some questions to get to know what he was thinking and feeling: "What's the hardest thing for you right now?" "What would make things look better to you?" "What do you not like about going to therapy?"
4. She could have named what she was observing to help him discover or discuss what was troubling him: "You seem so discouraged by not being able to walk. What's it like for you?" "Sometimes people in your kind of situation get frustrated at how slow improvement is. How is it for you?"

Choose a Solution

Judy decided to try the observation approach that is described in solution 4. She talked to Sidney about what she thought he might be experiencing, and he told her, "No, it isn't the walking that's so bad. It's everything else. It just seems I've lived too long. I've outlived most of my friends, and now with this stroke, it seems I'm outliving my health!"

By making her observation and by showing Sidney that she was interested in what he was thinking, Judy opened the door to a potentially rich conversation that might be healing for Sidney. Opportunities like this are not infrequent when you work with older persons.

Here are four suggestions for assisting patients during times of suffering:

- Inquire and listen.
- Avoid pat responses.
- Offer stories of faith to help find meaning.
- Use resources previously found helpful.

Inquire and Listen

When other people are experiencing turmoil it is healing to be able to listen to their expressions of feelings and thoughts, without judging or interrupting. They might ventilate anger and want you to just listen. They might feel sadness beyond words and want you just to be with them in silence. They might want you to affirm their acceptance of their burden.

They might ask questions such as the following without wanting you to answer, but they do want you to hear:

- "Why should I go on living?"
- "What use am I now? What good am I? I can't do anything."
- "I want to die. I'm a burden to my family."
- "It just doesn't make sense. Why me?"
- "How come God is punishing me?"
- "Don't tell me God is good when he took my daughter and left me, an old, worthless woman!"

You also need to be honest about your own feelings and thoughts. Feelings of inadequacy and powerlessness are common in the presence of people who are grappling with life's purpose and the role of suffering. You can't know the answers they are seeking. It is healing for you to admit that fact and to believe in the value of simply being with them during their searching.

Avoid Pat Responses

Quick phrases come readily to mind when you face someone who is hurting deeply. Yet such phrases as these are rarely helpful:

- "Good will come of it" misses the pain of the present moment; it may make the person feel that you really don't understand.

- "It's God's will" paralyzes; it effectively tells the older person that what they are feeling is insignificant.
- "Que sera, sera" or "That's fate" ignores the pain the person is experiencing.
- "It's no use crying over spilled milk" judges the person and tells him or her to stop feeling what he or she is feeling.
- "You shouldn't talk that way about God" judges the person, suggesting that what he or she is feeling or saying is wrong.
- "God must love you very much to send you such great suffering" distorts God's role and also misses the person's feelings; it implies that the person should be feeling gratitude when what he or she feels is pain.
- "Things could be worse" or giving an example of another's suffering trivializes the person's experience; it says that his or her problem really isn't all that important.
- "I know exactly how you feel" suggests the impossible; no one can know exactly how anyone else feels.

Pat phrases about suffering might be helpful to older persons who are suffering when they say them to themselves and when they fit their own viewpoints on the meaning of life and death. But even when an older person finds them to be true, he or she will rarely find it helpful to hear them from someone else.

Offer Stories of Faith to Help Find Meaning

Stories of faith can help an older person find meaning after the crisis and turmoil have subsided. John Shea, in *Stories of God*, talks about how people seek meaning in suffering and dying by interpreting the inexplicable through stories. Myths offer us a glimpse of how others made sense out of suffering and can give pointers on ways to behave when confronted with suffering.

You can share stories out of your own life experience, as well as the experiences of faith communities. Bible stories can help explain some of life's mysteries. Certain stories in literature offer rich descriptions of human beings responding to suffering and other life events. Stories like these don't explain away the unknown or minimize the individual's pain. They offer a framework for meeting it instead of hiding or running away from it.

For Mabel, it was remembering her mother. Whenever Mabel was having a particularly painful day with her arthritis, she would tell her roommate about her mother. "My mother had a hard life. She worked from morning to sunset on the homestead, even when she was almost crippled with arthritis. She'd sing, is what she'd do. And the more she hurt, the louder she'd sing. And us girls learned to try the same thing. And it helped. Now I sing in my mind when it hurts bad. And it still helps."

If you put current crises into a faith perspective and invite the sufferer to find ways to integrate the present with his or her spirituality, you may provide the key for the person to move from asking questions a victim asks to asking questions a person who wants to get the most out of each day asks, no matter what it might hold.

For example, Nancy, the nursing assistant, heard Mabel humming and noted the frown on Mabel's face. When she asked whether Mabel was in pain, Mabel said she was miserable. Nancy said, "When I'm finished here, I'll go talk to the nurse and ask about what we might be able to do for you. Tell me again about your mom and how she sang when she hurt."

In *When Bad Things Happen to Good People*, Harold Kushner describes the movement from "why" questions to "what now" and "how do I respond" questions. He describes the movement from feeling victimized to actively living in the present mystery. Turning to God to be judged or punished becomes turning to God or friends or even memories to be strengthened and comforted.

Use Resources Previously Found Helpful

When you least expect it, you might be the one who is with the older person when he or she is looking for strength. Many people who are struggling with meaning forget to look to the resources that have helped them throughout their lives. You could help by asking:

- "Is there someone you'd like to call to talk about this with?"
- "Have you been a member of a church or service club or other community during your life? Would someone from that group be helpful right now?"
- "Lots of times, people in situations like yours find it helpful to talk with someone like a minister or counselor or someone else who sees life from a perspective close to yours. How does that sound to you?"

- "You've lived through so many difficult times. What did you do in some of those other times that helped?"

Your questions might not yield answers, but they can plant a seed. Sometimes the resource might be a meal delivered by someone from church. It might be a visit with another person who shares similar beliefs. It might be a visit from a priest or rabbi or minister, or it might be the housekeeper or the nurse on the other side of the hall.

In summary, when the older person is asking questions that explore life's meaning, the sensitive listener will respect the search, avoid giving answers, and help look for the resources that proved helpful in times past.

Suggestions for Further Reading

American Psychiatric Association. *Diagnostic and Statistical Manual of Mental Disorders*, 3rd ed. rev. Washington, DC: APA, 1987.

Davidson, G. *Living with Dying*. Minneapolis: Augsburg Publishing, 1975.

Dunne, J. S. *Time and Myth: A Meditation on Storytelling As an Exploration of Life and Death*. London: University of Notre Dame Press, 1973.

Fischer, K. *Winter Grace: Spirituality for the Later Years*. New York City: Paulist Press, 1985.

Kubler-Ross, E. *On Death and Dying*. New York City: MacMillan, 1969.

Kushner, H. *When Bad Things Happen to Good People*. New York City: Avon Books, 1981.

Osgood, N. J. A systems approach to suicide prevention. *Psychotherapy and the Family* 5(1/2):117–31, 1989.

Rapp, S. R., Parisi, S. P., Walsh, D. A., and Wallace, C. E. Detecting depression in elderly medical inpatients. *Journal of Consulting and Clinical Psychology* 56:509–13, 1988.

Rovner, B. W., et al. Depression and mortality in nursing homes.

Journal of the American Medical Association 265(8):993–96 Feb. 27, 1991.

Shea, J. *Stories of God: An Unauthorized Biography*. London: St. Thomas More Press, 1978.

Schneidman, E. S., ed. *Death: Current Perspectives*, 2nd ed. Palo Alto, CA: Mayfield, 1980.

Afterword

Throughout this book, we have attempted to show how the most ordinary moments with an older person can be made into opportunities for satisfying conversations. The satisfaction is not one-sided; rather, both the older person and you, the caregiver, experience a feeling of being connected. You as a person have met the person who is the older patient. Such meetings can be unbelievably enriching.

We have explored some of the obstacles to easy conversation, whether they be in the older person or in us. Such barriers are sensory deficits, emotional pain, and patterns of interacting that tend to distance rather than attract. Suggestions have been offered for turning around difficult visits, respecting grief, challenging communication patterns, inviting memories, understanding silences, and exploring meaning and purpose.

Knowing what to say heals and mends. It creates stronger interactions between caregivers and elderly patients by opening the doors of discovery. Knowing what to say doesn't mean that conversation becomes effortless. If you find yourself having a difficult or empty conversation with an older person, you may have to be the one to bring more depth. It becomes your opportunity to view the older patient as a whole person with a rich and wonderful storehouse of history and wisdom. It becomes your sometimes difficult but usually rewarding task to take advantage of each interaction to ask real questions that call for real answers.

The result will be satisfaction — for both you and the person you are with, thus making the most of the time you have together.

Helping Patients Make Difficult Decisions

Chronic illnesses and health crises bring anguish to the elderly that need not be compounded. Exploring health care choices before a crisis arises and discussing such choices with sensitivity during times of crisis can lead to healing instead of adding to anguish.

Factors To Be Considered

Who and What

1. The patient and family should be central in the discussion.
2. The physician has primary responsibility for discussing diagnosis and prognosis and for making a recommendation about treatment options.
3. The physician, nurses, clergy, and others have responsibility for providing psychosocial and spiritual support and for explaining the medical information upon which decisions are based.

When

1. Ideally long before crisis
2. On admission to a health care facility
3. As disease progresses
4. During crises

Where

1. Patient's home
2. Physician's office
3. Health care facility
4. Any area that respects needs for privacy

Why

1. Respects moral right of patient to be primary decision maker
2. Provides control to patient
3. Assists families in knowing what their loved ones want

How

1. Communications should be timely, respectful, and clear; understanding needs to be validated.
2. Assessment should include:
   a. Meaning of illness
   b. Goals of health care
   c. Spiritual needs of patient
   d. Moral principles involved
      (1) A person has the moral obligation to use available procedures that offer a reasonable expectation of improving or maintaining health without creating serious burdens on self or significant others.
      (2) A person has the moral option to use or to refuse to use those procedures that either:
         (a) Do not offer reasonable expectation of maintaining or improving health
         (b) *Or* entail serious burdens for self or loved ones (pain, risk of injury/mortality, financial encumbrance)
3. *Examples* for starting the conversation include:
   - "We want to provide the best care possible for you. In order to do that, we need to know what *you* want."
   - "Have you thought about what kind of treatment you'd like if you were ever in a medical emergency?"
   - "What brought you here? How sick are you?"

- "Some people want the latest technological care available to prolong their lives; others want comfort measures. How about you?"
- "One of the things we want to assure you of is that we want to do what you would like us to do as we plan your care."
- "What kind of care would you like if you have an emergency or if you get really ill?"
- "We need to know what you would like us to do if your heart were to stop or if you stopped breathing. Have you thought about that? What have you thought?"
- "Have you talked with anyone in your family about this?"
- "If you're ever unable to make your own health care decisions, who would you like to make them for you?"

The words used aren't nearly as important as:

1. Talking with the patient as an adult
2. Being honest and direct
3. Asking open-ended questions
4. Being sensitive to the emotional impact of living with illness and the limits necessitating the current admission

Durable Power of Attorney for Health Care Decisions

The standard operating procedures of most health care facilities assume you as a patient would want life-sustaining procedures to be provided unless otherwise indicated. A durable power of attorney is a legal tool that you as an individual use to appoint another person to act on your behalf in case you are no longer capable or competent to do so yourself. The person appointed becomes and is called your attorney-in-fact or "agent" for health care decisions. This person is legally empowered specifically to make health care decisions for you when you can no longer do so.

You may pick anyone you like to make these decisions for you except your physician, any of your physician's employees, or an employee of a hospital or nursing home where you might become a patient. However, you may choose a person who is so employed if that person is related to you by blood, marriage or adoption. In fact, married people usually pick their husbands or wives.

Legislation in some states provides the following descending order of priority for decision makers for incapacitated patients:

1. The appointed guardian of the patient, if any
2. The individual, if any, to whom the patient has given durable power of attorney that encompasses the authority to make health care decisions
3. The patient's spouse
4. Children of the patient (children must be at least eighteen years of age)

5. Parents of the patient

6. Adult brothers and sisters of the patient

You may revoke your agent's authority at any time by simply telling or writing your physician or hospital. Remember, too, that your agent will make choices for you *only* if you become unable to do so.

Choosing Medical Care

After choosing your agent, you can also use the durable power of attorney to indicate the kinds of medical care you wish to receive and the kinds you don't want. You should talk over your preferences with your agent and your physician because they will cooperate to reach decisions in keeping with your preferences and medical condition.

Completing the Durable Power of Attorney

You can fill out the durable power of attorney without the services of an attorney. However, if you have any questions about this document, you should consult your attorney or your physician. In addition, you must sign this document in the presence of a notary public. (Your bank probably has a notary public who can notarize your signature.)

Keep your document with your other important papers, where it would be accessible to your agent. You should give a copy of the document to your agent and your physician.

DURABLE POWER OF ATTORNEY FOR HEALTH CARE

1. *Designation of Health Care Agent.* I, _____,
   do hereby designate and appoint the following persons, in the
   order listed, to serve as my Agent regarding health care decisions in my place in the event I am unable to give informed
   consent to decisions relating to such care due to my incapacity
   or incompetence as hereinafter defined. If the first person listed
   is unable or unwilling to serve, I appoint the second person.

   First Designee:

   Name: _____

   Address: _____

   _____

   Telephone: _____

   Second Designee:

   Name: _____

   Address: _____

   _____

   Telephone: _____

2. *Effectiveness.* This Durable Power of Attorney for Health Care
   shall become effective upon my inability to participate in my
   health care decisions, due to mental incapacity or incompetence or due to my mental or physical inability to communicate my instructions concerning my health care decisions.
   My incapacity or incompetence shall be determined by a
   physician who is familiar with my medical condition or by
   a court of competent jurisdiction. If determined by a physician, this Power of Attorney shall become effective when the
   physician has provided to my Agent(s) a written statement
   that I am incapacitated or incompetent.

3. *Powers Relating to Health Care Decisions.* My Agent for health care designated herein shall have all powers required to make health care decisions on my behalf, including giving informed consent to health care providers.

4. *Specific Directions.* Included in the power granted to my Agent is the authority to make decisions about life-prolonging medical procedures, such as (but not limited to) parenteral feeding, antibiotics, and cardiopulmonary resuscitation. My Agent may specifically request and concur with the writing of a "no-code" (DO NOT RESUSCITATE) order by my attending physician.

5. *Treatment in Event of Terminal Condition.* If I am diagnosed as having a terminal condition or as being permanently unconscious or in a persistent vegetative state, with no reasonable hope of recovery, or am diagnosed as having an incurable and irreversible condition which is not terminal but which causes me to experience severe and progressive physical or mental deterioration, I request that my Agent shall keep in mind my expressed wishes as indicated below by marking the applicable box next to **a. or b.** and by further marking my choice of **(1) or (2)** within those choices or by checking the box next to **c.** and specifying my directions therein. (I understand I should cross out any statement I do not agree with):

☐ a. I want my life to be prolonged to the greatest extent possible:

☐ (1) Without regard to the pain, discomfort, and other anticipated burdens that would be incurred, so long as there is chance for extending my life.

or

☐ (2) Unless, in my Agent's judgment, the anticipated pain, discomfort, or other burden of treatment outweighs its probable benefit. I want my Agent to consider the relief of suffering/pain and the quality as well as length of the possible extension of my life in making decisions about life-prolonging medical procedures.

OR

☐ b. I do not want any treatment that will merely prolong my dying. Thus, I want my treatment limited to medical and nursing measures that are intended to keep me comfortable, to relieve pain, and to maintain my dignity. In addition, if I am diagnosed as being permanently unconscious or in a persistent vegetative state, with no reasonable hope of recovery, I request that my Agent keep in mind my desires, as I have indicated below by checking one box:

- ☐ (1) I do not want medically assisted nutrition and hydration withheld or withdrawn from me.
- ☐ (2) I want medically assisted nutrition and hydration withheld or withdrawn from me.

☐ c. None of the above provisions shall apply to care. My directions concerning my care are as follows:

_____

_____

_____

_____

6. *Statement of Desires, Special Provisions, and Limitations.* In exercising the authority under this Durable Power of Attorney for Health Care, my Agent shall act consistently with my desires as stated above and as stated in any living will which I have executed which is in effect at the time of this Durable Power of Attorney. In addition, it is my wish that my Agent consider the following additional directions concerning my health care:

_____

_____

_____

_____

(Initial the statements that reflect your desires. Cross out the statements you *do not* agree with.)

7. *Consent to Organ Donation.* When my death has been legally determined, my Agent shall have the following described powers to consent to donate any needed organs, tissues, or parts of my body for purposes of transplantation or for anatomical study or medical school teaching:

☐ My Agent may donate such organs, etc., for the purpose of transplantation only;

☐ My Agent may donate such organs, etc., for purposes of transplantation and/or for anatomical study or medical school teaching.

☐ I do not wish my organs, tissues, or parts of my body donated for any purpose.

8. *Funeral and Burial.* I authorize my Agent to make any arrangements for my funeral and burial.

9. *Nomination of Guardians.* If protective proceedings for my person are ever commenced, I nominate the attorney-in-fact named herein as guardian of my person.

10. *Reliance.* A person acting without negligence and in good faith in reasonable reliance on this Durable Power of Attorney for Health Care and the apparent authority of the attorney-in-fact shall not incur any liability thereby. Any action so taken, unless otherwise invalid or unenforceable, shall be binding on my heirs and personal representatives.

11. *Harmless.* My estate shall hold harmless and indemnify the attorney-in-fact from all liability for acts done in good faith and not in fraud of me.

12. *Applicable Law.* The laws of the State of _____ shall govern this Durable Power of Attorney for Health Care.

13. *Prior Designations Revoked.* I revoke any prior Durable Power of Attorney for Health Care.

I sign my name to this Durable Power of Attorney for Health Care on the _____ day of _____, 19_____, at

_____, _____.

_____

Address: _____

_____

STATE OF _____)

                      : ss.

County of _____)

     On this _____ day of _____, 1991, personally appeared before me _____, to me known to be the individual described in and who executed the within and foregoing instrument, and acknowledged that _____ (he/she) signed the same as _____ (his/her) free and voluntary act and deed, for the uses and purposes therein mentioned.

     GIVEN UNDER my hand and official seal the day and year in this certificate first above written.

                                   _____

                                   Notary Public in and for the State of

                                   _____, residing at _____

                                   _____

                                   My Commission Expires: _____

Chapter Outlines

The following outlines were designed for use in one-hour-long in-service educational sessions organized around the subject matter of each chapter.

Chapter 1—Developing Communication Skills

I. Introduction
   A. If we improve conversation with elderly patients we will see:
      1. Reduction of stress as caregivers
      2. Reduction of stress in patients
      3. Improved patient cooperation
      4. Increased enjoyment of work
   B. As a group, discuss other possible benefits.
II. Beginning Conversations
   A. Read and discuss the three techniques for beginning conversations.
      1. Focus on patient's physical and emotional state. Do exercise 1-1.
      2. Give patient your total attention, show interest, structure your time, and clarify your purpose. Do exercises 1-2 and 1-3.
      3. Ask open-ended questions. Discuss additional open-ended questions (such as those on p. 11) your group used or heard. Show you are listening by what you do as well as say.
      4. Do exercises 1-4 through 1-7.

III. Concluding Conversations
   A. Discuss ending of chapter.
   B. Share conversation endings you have seen or heard that leave both parties satisfied.
IV. Summarize by Reviewing the Chapter Divisions

Chapter 2—Conveying Respect

I. Introduction
   A. Two factors erode respect of older persons:
      1. Ageism in our society: an attitude that implies that old people are somehow worth less than younger people
      2. Attitudes and behaviors of some older people that can get in the way of easy, satisfying conversation
   B. Four areas that can impede conveying respect:
      1. Marked control of territory
      2. Mild confusion
      3. Inflexible or patterned life-style
      4. Unnecessary dependence or unrealistic independence
   C. Do exercise 2-1.
II. Territoriality
   A. Exaggerated attention to territory and ownership can be a symptom of feeling one has very little control in other areas of life.
   B. Situations requiring sensitivity to territorial concerns:
      1. A new living situation
      2. A move to a "home"
      3. Increased necessity for physical contact
      4. Expressions of paranoia
   C. Do exercise 2-2.
III. Mild Confusion
   A. Intermittent confusion can be minimized by following these suggestions:
      1. Assume that the person wants to function in the present.
      2. Gently remind the person what is real.
      3. Be specific when describing people and situations.
      4. Use remote memory to pull the person back to the present.
      5. Use visual aids to provide clarity and affirm reality.

6. Be true to your word.
    B. Do exercises 2-3 and 2-4.
IV. Inflexibility
    A. People age as they have lived their lives, some eager for new experiences, others preferring predictability.
    B. Do exercise 2-5.
    C. Show respect by getting to know the patient as a person. Questions that recall an earlier life-style can be helpful.
V. Dependence and Independence
    A. Who is this person?
        1. Assess how independently or dependently the person lived prior to coming to your care by asking family members.
        2. Assess how much independence is desired by direct questions.
    B. Choices about care should be offered to the patient as long as he or she is able to make decisions.
        1. Treatment choices, such as DNR orders, hospitalization, surgery
        2. Daily living choices, such as meal partner, use of free time, schedule for awakening
    C. Exercise: With a partner, role-play interviewing a new patient about advance directives. Ask questions such as "Have you thought about what kind of care you would want if you got sicker?" "Who would you want to help make decisions if you became unable to do so?" "What have you told your doctor about these things?" "Have you prepared a durable power of attorney for health care decisions?"
VI. Conclusion: You're in a pivotal position to enhance the patient's remaining independence or foster dependence, to give control rather than to take control, and to model caring even when it's difficult.

Chapter 3—Turning Challenges into Opportunities

I. Introduction
    A. Discuss communication challenges.
        1. Misunderstanding of memories
        2. Inappropriate parenting remarks

      3. Lack of awareness of your own reactions to the patient
      4. Patient's communication impairments
  B. Discuss two or more reactions to communication challenges.
      1. Stop talking.
      2. Visit less frequently.
      3. Get angry.
      4. Other ideas: _____

II. Building Conversation through Memories
  A. Think of ways memories are important to you.
  B. Do exercise 3-1.
  C. Recall some memories of patients and how you responded to those memories.
  D. Do exercise 3-2.

III. Caregivers' Reactions to Communication Challenges
  A. Read the story of Cindy.
  B. Do exercise 3-3.

IV. "Parenting" Remarks
  A. Read the story of Mr. Roderio.
  B. What are the most important things he says?
  C. Do exercise 3-4.

V. Understanding Communication Impairments
  A. Do exercise 3-5 and discuss the results.
  B. Do exercise 3-6 and discuss the results.

VI. Summarize by Reviewing the Main Chapter Divisions
  A. Do exercise 3-7.

Chapter 4 — Exploring Meaning and Purpose in Living

I. Introduction
  A. Grief is part of everyone's life. It is the natural response to the loss of someone or something significant.
  B. Gentle assistance with grieving helps a person maintain a sense of meaning and purpose even with significant losses.
  C. Do exercises 4-1 and 4-2.

II. Individuality of Grief
  A. Group exercise:
      1. Individually complete exercise 4-3.
      2. In groups of three, share answers to numbers 1, 2, 5, and 8.

3. Debrief in whole group, noting similarities, differences, points that surprised the participants.
   B. Each loss is experienced uniquely; comparisons and explanations are usually not helpful.
III. Patterns of Grieving
   A. Grief typically has five phases:
      1. Anticipatory—that preceding an expected loss
      2. Immediate—right after the loss
      3. Emotion-laden—in the several days after the loss
      4. Disorganization—a varying period of deep sadness and withdrawal
      5. Reintegration—putting life back together and finding ways to discover satisfaction again
   B. Sensitive response from other people can help heal the grief. Exercise:
      1. Recall a grief experience out of your own past.
      2. Write down two things people did or said that you found helpful.
      3. In small group, share your answers to #2, above.
   C. Do exercise 4-1.
   D. Discuss specific aspects of older persons' grieving:
      1. Cumulative losses can increase the intensity of the grief response.
         a. Do exercise 4-2.
      2. Lack of living confidants reduces opportunities for sharing.
      3. Grief can mask depression.
         a. Patients should be evaluated routinely for clinical depression.
         b. Caregivers should know the symptoms of clinical depression.
IV. Spirituality and Suffering
   A. Spirituality is the process of living what one believes.
   B. Because everyone is unique, it requires inquiry to discover what counts for another person.
      1. Group exercise: in groups of three:
         a. Ask two of the following questions:
            • "Where have you found strength when you've been discouraged?"
            • "Who have you looked up to? Who inspires you?"
            • "What does dying mean to you?"

- "What does suffering mean to you?"
- "With whom do you share your innermost dreams?"
- "How does this experience fit into your picture of life?"

  b. Debrief large group.

  2. Third-person observations practice. With a partner, role-play the scenario on p. 87 with Sidney and his therapy aide Judy. If you were Judy, what would you say? And how do you think Sidney would respond?

C. Helpful responses:
  1. Inquire and listen.
  2. Avoid pat responses.
  3. Share own sources of meaning.
  4. Use resources previously helpful to person.

V. Conclusion: Caring for people during times of grieving or the search for meaning is simple yet delicate. It is a privilege to share such moments with another person. You might be the right person at the right time to bring healing, helping the person turn from "Why me?" to "Where do I go from here?"

Model Answers for Exercises

Model Answers for Exercise 1-1, Initiating a Conversation

Here are two sample answers:

1. "Good morning, Mrs. Goodman. Your coloring is much better this morning than it was yesterday. How do you feel?"
2. "Hello, Mr. Beasley. [Hold up his hearing aid.] Here is your hearing aid. Would you like me to help you put it in? Now, how much rest did you get last night?"

Model Answers for Exercise 1-2, Showing Respect

1. "That covers the list of questions I wanted to ask. Is there something you're wondering about?"
2. Asking permission to sit on edge of bed
3. Leaning toward the patient and holding her or his hand
4. "It's good to see you again. What can I do for you?"
5. "I'm glad to see your appetite is back. Maybe at lunch I can stop by for a couple of minutes."

Model Answers for Exercise 1-3, Communicating in Special Situations

A. "While I'm doing this, could you tell me more about your problem?"
B. "I know you want your medical treatment now, but first, this information will help us know about your improvement. The nurse will be here in about 30 minutes."

C. "I have an emergency, but I want to come back afterward and help you."

D. "I really want to read your letter, but I'm a little behind schedule. Can I come back during my break about 10:30 to see it?"

Model Answers for Exercise 1-4, Recognizing Feelings

1. "You're unhappy here."
2. "You wish he'd write you. You seem sad about it."
3. "You're afraid. What happened last visit?"
4. "You are finally feeling better! Good."

Model Answers for Exercise 1-5, Understanding Silences

"Good morning, Mrs. Anderson. You usually say 'hi.' What's happened? Are you in some discomfort? I'll just finish here. Would you like me to come back later for a visit?"

Model Answers for Exercise 1-6, Recognizing What Stops Conversations

1. Judges patient
2. Assumes the complaint is not valid
3. Ignores pain
4. Ignores pain
5. Assumes worse will happen and judges patient
6. Shows lack of interest and judges patient

Model Answers for Exercise 1-7, Relating How to Relate

Shows lack of interest:

1. Looking at watch
2. Edging toward door
3. Not answering

Shows interest:

1. Leaning toward you
2. Ignoring outside distractions (for example, television)
3. Sitting down beside you

Model Answers for Exercise 2-1, Offering Control

Possible answers (there could be *many* helpful answers):

1. "There are two rooms available. Let me tell you about each of the roommates and you can decide which sounds better for you."
2. "There's a concert in the cafeteria. Would you like to go? It's the choir from Holman School. You enjoyed them last year when they visited."

Model Answers for Exercise 2-4, Dealing with Confusion

1. "I'm your nurse, Kathy. You must be thinking of Marie this morning. It's been three years since she died. What were you recalling?"
2. "Does it seem like I wasn't here this morning? It was a very short visit—I came in right after you woke up and helped you with your clothes."

Model Answers for Exercise 3-2, Responding to Memory Sharing

Here are sample answers for the three statements:

1. "Yes, just yesterday you said that. Do you remember what she looked like when she was a baby?" (This uses memory as a bridge to other information and tells her you have heard that statement before.)
2. "You wish things could have stayed the same. What decade did you really like the best, the thirties or the fifties?" (This approach uses a cue—past years—to ask a new question.)
3. "Yes, you've told me. When was your first marriage?" (This uses memory as a bridge to other information.)

Model Answers for Exercise 3-4, Offering Choices

Here are sample statements for each category:

1. Health—"Would you like to go to bed a little earlier tonight?"
2. Time—"Would you like to sit outside or go in to crafts?"

3. Clothing—"Is this still comfortable or would you prefer the other dress?"
4. Diet—"Would you like to have some tea while you're waiting?"
5. Living choices—"We could move you to the room with the view over the trees now. Would you like that or prefer to stay here?"

Model Answers for Exercise 4-1, Exploring Grief

1. "What did you hear from the doctor?" "How are you doing with the latest news about your chemo?"
2. "How could you tell?" "What did you notice?"
3. "Put your hand on his and ask him, 'What's wrong?'"

Model Answer for Exercise 4-2, Dealing with Loss

Nurse: "I know you hate it. What's the hardest thing about going?"

Sidney: "It just reminds me how helpless I am! You can walk. You couldn't know how hard it is to be unable to do so!"

Nurse: "You're right. I can't imagine. You must feel really frustrated. What did you used to do when you were going through hard times?"

3031